WINNING GOLF
Made Easy

WINNING GOLF
Made Easy

Johnny M. Anderson

 Sterling Publishing Co., Inc.   New York

Library of Congress Cataloging-in-Publication Data Available

10   9   8   7   6   5   4   3   2   1

First published in the United States in 1992
by Sterling Publishing Company, Inc.
387 Park Avenue South, New York, N.Y. 10016
Published in Great Britain in 1992
by A & C Black (Publishers) Limited
as *Golf Made Easy*
35 Bedford Row, London WC1R 4JH
World copyright © 1992 Streiffert & Co.
Box 6334, S-102 46 Stockholm, Sweden
Distributed in Canada by Sterling Publishing
% Canadian Manda Group, P.O. Box 920, Station U
Toronto, Ontario, Canada M8Z 5P9
Color reproduction: Repro-Man, Gothenburg, Sweden
Printed in Italy
All rights reserved

Sterling ISBN 0-8069-8402-3

CONTENTS

INTRODUCTION

No matter what anybody else says to you, you play golf to enjoy yourself and have fun out there on the course. No more, no less. The more you improve, the more you will enjoy yourself. And remember, it is against the course and your own handicap that you play, not against your golf partners.

The object of the game of golf is to play the course on any given day under the prevailing circumstances in the lowest possible number of shots, while you are really enjoying yourself.

You can improve your game!
Everybody can improve their game. Thirty-five years spent teaching golf to beginners, high- and low-handicap golfers, international players, and professionals, have taught me that. Another thing those years have taught me is that practice does not make perfect, but that only *intelligent* practice will improve your game and your

enjoyment of it. Furthermore, my experience is that there is no substitute for good tuition, so this book is intended to be a complement to the lessons you get from your pro. It can be used also at any time to refresh your memory and to help you improve your scoring.

The more you learn about golf, the greater your understanding of the game; the more you understand, the greater your golfing confidence; and the more confident you are about your golf, the greater are your chances of success. This book is a step-by-step approach to building up a solid golf game and will help you to improve by taking one step at a time, never moving forwards until the previous step has been understood, practised and mastered.

Step by step

This book is designed to help all those golf players who are not satisfied with the way their game is developing. Beginners will find that the easy-to-follow photographs and instructions will be an excellent aid when they are going through the basics or want to refresh their minds on lessons they have received from their golf instructor. More experienced players will be able to refer to the relevant section when they find that a particular part of their game seems to have deteriorated.

The aim is to help you to build up and improve your game step by step, starting with putting and then going through chipping, pitching, the half swing, the three-quarter swing, and finally the full swing. Do not go on to a new section before you are sure that the previous one has been understood and practised success-fully, thus giving you the confidence to break new ground.

Don't make it so difficult!

Golf must be the most frustrating and difficult ball game devised, so you should always try to keep it as simple as possible. All beginners and even those who have played for a considerable time have a tendency to make it more difficult than it really is. The reasons for this follow.

1 Lack of understanding: you don't quite know what you are trying to do with your golf swing. The object of the golf swing is to strike the ball with the club face and swing path pointing at the target at the moment of impact. No more, no less.

2 Bad memory or loss of emotional control: you forget your all-important pre-swing routine or you get angry at or frightened by a particular situation.

3 You try too hard: inexperienced weekend players try to imitate the speed, agility and strength of the tournament players who practise and play every day.

4 Not enough intelligent practice: after a golf lesson from your pro, you prefer to get out on the course and play badly than to stay in the practice area and improve your game by intelligent practice.

Practice

Playing high- or middle-handicap golf has as little to do with professional tournament golf as driving a family car in town has to do with Formula 1 racing. Professional tournament golfers are top athletes and are not easily copied. They practise and play regularly. When they practise, they work at one particular aspect of their game, concentrating on one type of shot only, taking their time at it, and noting the results.

High-handicap players usually practise with the wooden clubs, and to the bystander they sometimes look like windmills trying to hit as many balls as possible into the air at the same time. When you practise, start with your shorter shots and take your time. Consider each shot you take and try to work out why it went the way it did. Write it down in a notebook that you should always have with you. Then at the end of the session, summarise the results of your practice shots, so that you can refer to them at the start of your next practice session.

CHAPTER ONE
EQUIPMENT AND GEOMETRY FOR THE GOLFER

As we are all built differently, golf clubs are particularly individual and should be chosen with care. A club that does not suit your style of play or your physical ability will make it very difficult for you to improve at the game. There are many different shaft flexes and club-head weights to choose from; if you are a normal weekend golfer or middle-handicapper, you are simply not knowledgeable enough to choose for yourself. Instead, turn to the golf pro who has had the privilege of teaching you – there is no better person to help you choose clubs that are right for you, your physique, your style of playing, and the degree of improvement that he or she expects you to attain.

THE CLUBS

As a rule, stiff-shafted and heavy-headed clubs are best left to the strong and experienced playing professionals. You, as a high- or medium-handicapper, need clubs that will give you a better chance of making a high percentage of good golf shots, while giving you the best possible results from your bad shots.

According to the rules of golf, you may not play with more than fourteen clubs in your bag, and professionals always choose their fourteen to suit the prevailing weather conditions and the particular course to be played.

The beginner will probably improve faster if he or she uses only the Nos 3, 5 and 7 woods and the Nos 5, 7 and 9 irons, the pitching wedge, the sand iron and the putter. Using the full set before you are experienced enough will only be confusing and will lead to uncertainty and lack of confidence.

Which club to use?
The use of the clubs is fairly obvious. The longer-shafted clubs send the ball further. The woods are for shots from the tee or for the 'transport' shots that should leave you with a simple shot on to the green, close to the flag. The No. 3 wood is used from the tee, while the Nos 5 and 7 woods are for play on the fairway or for par 3 tee shots. Shots hit with these clubs allow you a greater margin of error – for instance, ball side-spin will be less than with the driver, so there will be a minimum loss of line (direction) and length.

The middle irons are for playing the ball on to the green with a reasonable amount of accuracy. The No. 5 iron is the longest iron the high-handicapper can use with any accuracy, so leave the longer irons until you can handle them properly.

Use the shorter clubs when accuracy is at a premium; in other words, when you want to send the ball higher and shorter to land on the green. The pitching wedge (or 'wedge', as it is also known) is for play near

the green, while the sand iron is, as the name indicates, for playing from sand, but it is also a useful weapon when you need to get out of troublesome rough or when you need extra height to your shot. Finally, the putter is for playing the ball in the vicinity of the flag.

Here I have placed the clubs correctly in their bag, which is big enough to hold extra clothing and other necessities. I always keep the woods protected with head covers.

Opposite is my present set of clubs:
three woods (Nos 1, 3 and 5), nine irons (Nos 3 – 9, a pitching wedge and a sand iron), and one putter. You will notice that the more lofted the club, the shorter the shaft.

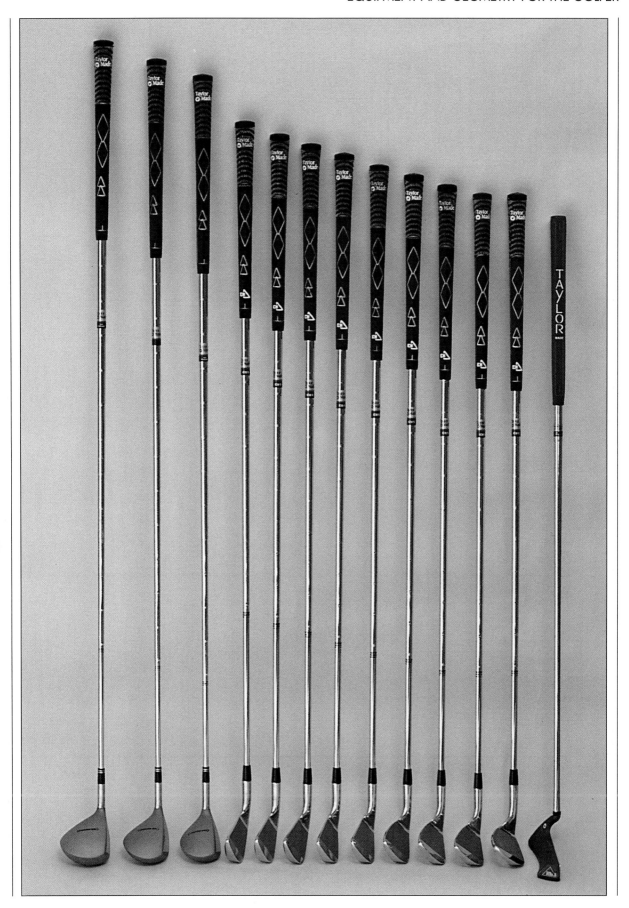

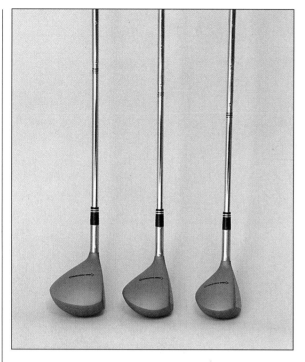

The metal woods – from left to right, the No. 1 (driver), 3 and 5. Woods are made from No. 1 – 7 and should be chosen to suit your personal style of playing. Note that the more lofted the club, the shallower the club face. (Compare the No. 5 to the No. 1 wood.)

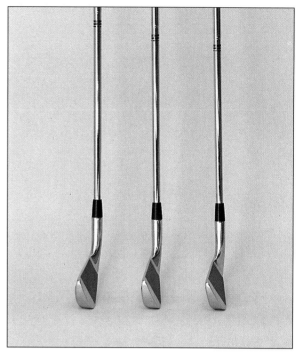

The thin-bladed and less lofted irons – from left to right, the No. 3, 4 and 5 – are used to send the ball a considerable distance.

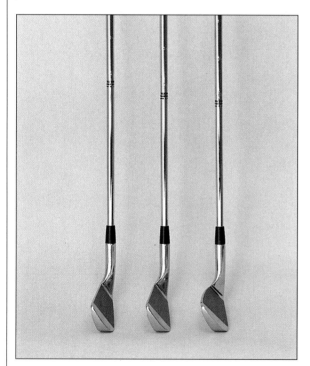

The medium irons – from left to right, the No. 6, 7 and 8 – are used for shots from about 140 yds (130 m) in to the green, but can also be used for chipping on to the green.

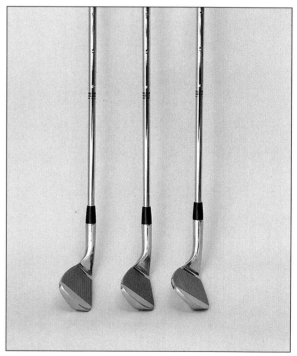

The short irons – from left to right, the No. 9 iron, the pitching wedge and the sand iron – are the precision clubs. They have plenty of loft, which creates height and back-spin.

THE PUTTER

There are several types of putter on the market today, the most popular being the blade putter, the centre-shafted putter, and the mallet-headed putter. Which type you use is a matter of personal preference, but the following points are important.

Lie
The lie of the club must be correct, i.e. when the complete sole of the club is resting flat on the ground the angle of the shaft to the body is such that by leaning only slightly forwards your eyes are immediately over and just behind the ball.

Length of shaft
The length of the shaft must be such that you do not have to crouch or stand abnormally upright.

Appearance
The putter must look and feel easy to use, with an easily found sweet spot, thus creating confidence, which is so important to good putting.

Feel
A good putter will feel well balanced and will want to swing itself after the backswing.

A good putter will have a sharply defined front edge, giving you a clear indication of the intended line. If you feel unsure, ask your local professional for advice.

CARE OF CLUBS

Keep your clubs in good condition. When they get dirty, clean the club heads in soapy water, paying special attention to the grooves. Dry them carefully after washing. The rubber grip should not be shiny or hard, as this will make you hold the club too tightly, causing unnecessary tension. If the rubber grip is in bad condition, have it replaced by your professional.

Use head covers for the woods – even for the metal woods. Remember that clubs that are well looked after will not only last longer but will also assist you in playing better.

The most commonly used putter on the professional tour today is the centre-shafted putter, in which the shaft is more or less centred in the head.

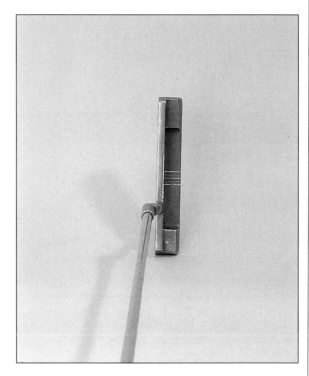

The position of the sweet spot is indicated by the lines on the top of the club head.

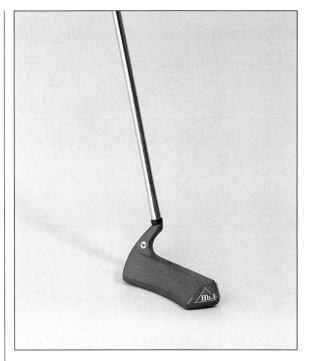

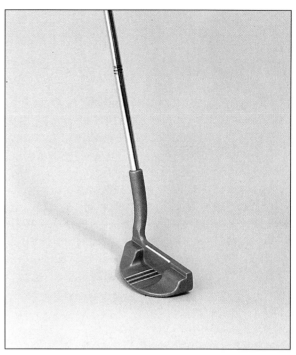

The modern blade putter has its shaft joining the club head at the heel.

The mallet-headed putter has a pronounced flange at the back of the blade.

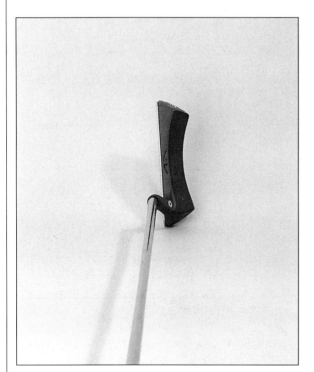

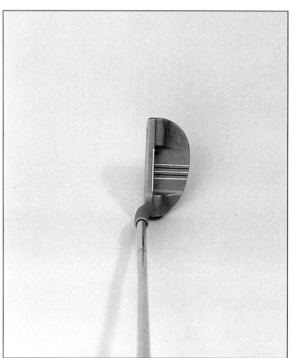

The sweet spot is indicated by marks just behind the front edge of the blade. (*Above*)

The sweet spot of the mallet-headed putter is shown by lines on the flange. (*Above right*)

Note that all three putters have so-called 'goose necks', which ensure that at address the hands are just in front of the blade, which helps to prevent the putter head from arriving at the ball before the hands, sending the ball to the left.

Accessories

A bag with plenty of space for extra clothing, a water bottle, and perhaps a refreshing snack (a sandwich and some fruit) is a sound investment. A smaller bag, for carrying a reduced number of clubs, is also a good buy. The big bag can be used when you play a full round with a complete set of clubs. It is then a good idea to have a trolley for your bag, since walking 4–5 miles (6–8 km) and playing golf is tiring enough without having to carry a heavy bag. The small bag will serve for playing just a few holes in the evening or when you go to the practice area.

Whether you use a golf glove is a matter of personal preference. The majority of professionals wear golf gloves except when putting. Many players find that it gives them a better grip and, therefore, increased confidence during the swing.

The type of golf shoes you choose will depend on what type of course you play most frequently, but whatever kind of shoes you have, keep them in good condition. Replace worn spikes and fit shoe trees when you are not using your shoes. If you play a good deal of golf, it is wise to have two pairs of shoes in order to allow one pair to 'rest up' while you are using the other. If you play in a rainy climate, a pair of rubber golf boots is a boon, keeping your feet and legs dry, especially if you spend plenty of time in the rough.

Buy twenty or thirty practice balls of good quality for practising your chipping and putting, because driving-range balls do not generate the correct sensation felt when playing good shots around and on the green.

The best teacher

Let me now introduce you to the finest and most honest golf teacher in the world. It is *always* with you when you are playing, it cannot lie, and it does only what you tell it to, without asking questions. This trustworthy teacher is none other than your golf ball. It can do only what is achieved with your influence. If you strike

it cleanly using a full swing, it will do one of nine things in relation to the target line, and it will never do anything else. The target line is the imaginary line that runs back from the target through the ball; we will refer to the target line frequently throughout this book, so if this basic definition is not already firmly imprinted on your mind, make a point of imprinting it now. The nine ball-flight alternatives are the following.

1 The ball will fly in a straight line towards the target.

2 It will fly in a straight line to the left of the target. This is known as a **pull**.

3 It will fly in a straight line to the right of the target. This is a **push**.

4 It will start off straight and then curve slightly to the left. A **draw**.

5 It will start off straight and then curve slightly to the right. A **fade**.

6 It will start off to the left of the target line and then curve to the right. A **pull-slice**.

7 It will start off to the left of the target line and then curve even more to the left. A **pull-hook**.

8 It will start off to the right of the target line and then curve to the left. A **push-hook**.

9 It will start off to the right of the target line and then curve even more to the right. A **push-slice**.

Swing path at impact

According to the coaching books, points 1 to 3 above indicate the effect of the club head's swing path at impact. The swing path is the line followed by the club head during the swing and it is always referred to in relation to the target line. The correct swing path is in-to-along-to-in, that is from the inside (your side) of the target line on the downswing, along the target line just before and after impact, and then back inside the target line on the upswing/follow through. Any other swing path will not start the ball off on a straight line towards the target.

The alignment of the club face at impact

The coaching books also tell you that a ball that curves after starting off straight indicates that the swing path was correct. However, the club face at impact was not square to the target line, but either open or closed to varying degrees (points 4 and 5). Points 6 to 9 are all caused by club faces that were not square to the swing path at impact. The fact that the ball did not start straight at the target tells you that the swing path was incorrect.

The angle of approach of the club head to the ball

Furthermore, the coaching books will tell you, the steepness of the downswing (the angle at which the club face approaches the ball) will affect the length and height of the ball's flight. A ball struck by a club head that is approaching too steeply will lose some length and gain more height than if it was hit by a club head swinging down at the normal angle of approach. If we add to this a club face that is open, the ball will fly even higher.

Cause and effect

So, how does the ordinary golfer learn the ins and outs of ball-flight laws without taking out a degree in Golf Engineering? Don't be put off by the technicalities; it is basically quite straightforward. The important thing is to think of the golf swing as a simple cause-and-effect phenomenon (your swing will cause an effect on the ball, i.e. it will make it do one of the nine things listed above). The table at the bottom of the page will show you this cause-and-effect approach more simply.

Whenever your shot does not succeed in making the ball finish up where you wanted it to go, you know that you have done something wrong. The flight of the ball shows you what it was that you did, so you can then concentrate on correcting the error (or errors). How to do this is described on p. 141.

EFFECT	CAUSE
1 The ball flies in a straight line towards the target.	You have done everything right unless you didn't want to hit that ball straight towards the target! In other words, the swing path was from the inside of the target line to along it at impact and then back inside, with the club face square at impact.
2 It flies in a straight line to the left of the target.	You have done everything right except that the club face travelled from outside the target line on the downswing to inside the target line on the follow through (known as out-to-in).
3 It flies in a straight line to the right of the target.	You have done everything right except that the club face travelled on a path that went from inside the target line on the downswing to outside the target line on the follow through (known as an in-to-out swing path).
4 It starts off straight to the target and then curves to the left.	You have swung the club to the target but the club face was closed at impact.
5 It starts off straight to the target and then curves to the right.	You have swung the club to the target but the club face was open at impact.
6 It starts off to the left of the target line and then curves back to the right.	This time, your swing path was out-to-in and the club face was open to the swing path at impact. Two things to correct!
7 It starts off to the left of the target line and then curves more to the left.	Your swing path was out-to-in and the club face was closed to the swing path at impact. Again, two things to correct.
8 It starts off to the right of the target line and then curves back to the left.	Your swing path was in-to-out and the club face was closed to the swing path at impact. Two things to correct.
9 It starts off to the right of the target line and then curves to the right.	Your swing path was in-to-out and the club face was open to the swing path at impact. Two things to correct.

The ball-flight alternatives

The flight of the ball will tell you if you need to adjust your swing. Quite simply, the ball tends to start in the direction of the swing path and finish in the direction of the club-face position at impact.

1. At impact, the swing path and the position of the club head were correct, resulting in a straight shot towards the target.

2. At impact, the position of the club face was square to the swing path, but the swing path was out-to-in, resulting in a straight shot to the left.

3. Again, club-face position was square to the swing path, but the swing path was in-to-out, resulting in a straight shot to the right.

4. The swing path was correct but the club face was closed at impact, so that the ball curves to the left after starting off straight towards the target.

5. The swing path was correct but the club face was open at impact, so the ball curves to the right after starting off straight toward the target.

6. The swing path was out-to-in and the club face was open to the swing path at impact, so the ball started off to the left and then curved to the right.

7. The swing path was out-to-in and the club face was closed to the swing path at impact, so the ball started off to the left and then curved more to the left.

8. The swing path was in-to-out and the club face was closed to the swing path at impact, so the ball started off to the right of the target line and then curved back to the left.

9. The swing path was in-to-out and the club face open to the swing path at impact, so the ball started off to the right and then curved more to the right.

CHAPTER
TWO
PUTTING

Smart people start with the putter!
The intelligent approach to learning golf is to start at
the beginning – with putting. You cannot expect to
strike a ball straight and true 150 yds/m in the air if
you are not able to putt it so that it rolls a short
distance along the ground to the hole.
So let's start correctly and
achieve success from the beginning.

THE ART OF PUTTING

The idea behind putting is simply to get the ball in the hole. To be regularly successful at this, the ball must be struck by the club's sweet spot, with a slight accelerating movement towards the target and with enough speed for the ball to reach the hole. The sweet-spot strike gives the ball a more controlled direction and distance.

It is difficult to over-emphasise the importance of putting – ironically the most under-practised part of most players' game. It appears so simple to roll a ball along the ground towards a target, that beginners prefer to practise the 'harder' parts of the game, the drive, the long irons, and so on. Furthermore, many golfers find it difficult to believe that putting should be done in a specific manner. Perhaps this is because professional players appear to putt in a wide variety of ways. This may be so, but there are certain putting basics which all golf players (pros included) must take into account, and we cover these in the following pages. The intelligent golfer is the one who works constantly at perfecting the art of putting, with these basics in mind.

The putter

1. There are a number of differences between the iron clubs and the putter. Firstly, there is very little loft on the putter – loft would lift the ball and the object of putting is to make the ball *roll* along the ground. Secondly, there are no markings on the face of the putter – markings help create back-spin, which is to be avoided in the putt. Thirdly, the angle at which the shaft enters the club head is more perpendicular than that of any of the other clubs (this enables you to have your eyes directly over the putting line without having to lean too far forwards).

2. Even the grip is different. Its shape is different and the part on which you place your thumbs is flattened and thickened towards the top, enabling you to hold the club in a manner designed to increase precision. Also, the material of the grip is different – it gives a softer 'feel'.

3. If you place the head of the putter flat on the ground beside that of any other club, you will see that the putter head is much nearer your feet and the shaft more upright, enabling you to stand closer to the ball.

4. How to find the sweet spot. Hold the shaft near the head and tap it with a tee, starting at the toe and working your way towards the heel. When the club head no longer twists but swings back and forwards, you have found the sweet spot.

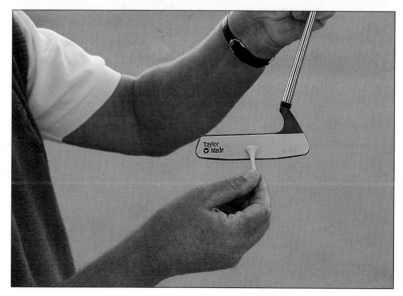

THE PUTTING GRIP

There are several ways of holding a putter and most golf players have, at some time in their golfing lives, tried some of them in an attempt to improve their putting. We show three of the most usual grips here. Each golfer should pick the grip that feels most comfortable and gives the best results.

The reverse overlap grip
This is the most usual grip. Hold the putter mainly with the last three fingers of each hand, with the left hand nearer the top of the shaft. The forefinger of the left hand is placed outside the last three fingers of the right hand. Three things should then point straight at the target: the back of the left hand, the face of the club head, and the palm of the right hand. This position helps to reduce wrist movement while allowing the arms to control the amount and direction of the movement. If your putting is causing you problems, it may be because your wrists are still hingeing; counteract this by turning the hands away from one another a little.

The standard grip, used by most players, is known as the reverse overlap grip.

The reverse overlap grip

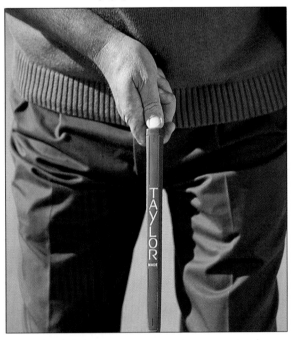

1. Hold the very top of the putter in your right hand with the full area of its sole in contact with the ground and the shaft upright or even forward.

2. Place the left hand so that its lifeline is along the leading edge of the shaft. The back of the left hand should then point in the same direction as the club face.

3. Put your left thumb perpendicularly along the flattened top of the shaft and fold your fingers round it, holding the shaft against the palm of your hand with the pressure coming mostly from the last three fingers.

4. Place your right hand on the shaft, holding the club at the junction of the fingers and the hand, with all four fingers on the shaft. The palm of the right hand should be facing in the same direction as the club face too.

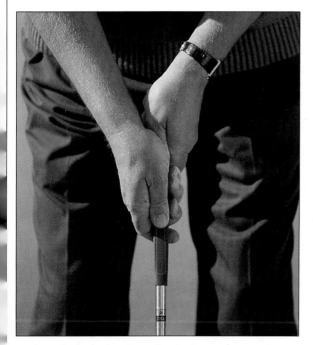

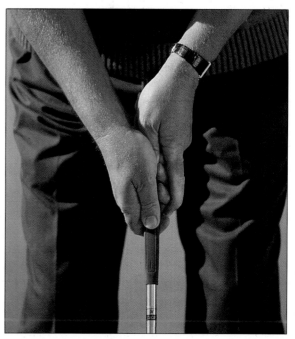

5. Place the right thumb on the shaft, snugly over the top of the left thumb. Both thumbs are placed on the flattened part of the grip and are arched (not stretched). Keep the pressure in the right hand light, and coming mostly from the last three fingers.

6. Remove your left forefinger from the shaft and place it outside the fingers of the right hand, to stabilise the back of your left wrist. It may lie pointing absolutely straight down or it may be slightly curled.

The full ten-finger grip

In the full ten-finger putting grip, all ten fingers are on the shaft, and the thumbs are perpendicular. The pressure comes from the last three fingers of both hands. The right forefinger may be laid along the side of the shaft, if it feels better, but remember to keep the pressure constant. For some reason, this grip is also known as the 'over-40 grip', even though some great young players use it with excellent results.

The cross-handed or upside-down grip

As in the grip just described, all ten fingers are on the shaft in the cross-handed grip, with the thumbs again perpendicular. This time, however, the left hand is placed beneath the right.

This grip is becoming popular among senior players (even senior professionals) as they find it easier to keep the face of the putter square at contact, as they pull the club through the ball with the lower left arm.

The three grip positions just described all do the same thing: they eliminate unnecessary wrist movement during the stroke. Wrist movement is almost always detrimental to good putting, so a backward and forward pendulum, or one-lever, movement caused only by the arms will give you the best and most consistent results.

No matter which of the three grips is chosen, the pressure exerted should be firm and constant throughout the stroke. The further you are from the hole, the firmer you hold the club.

The full ten-finger grip ————

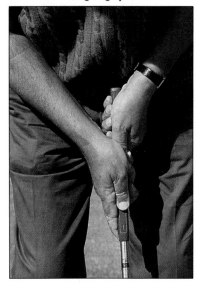

Searching for increased sensitivity, some players find the full ten-finger grip to be best. The routine is exactly the same as for the reverse overlapping grip (1– 6, pp. 22–3) but with all the fingers of the left hand on the shaft. If you wish, the right forefinger may be extended down the shaft.

The cross-handed grip ————

The cross-handed grip has been adopted by many professionals in an effort to improve scoring.

1. The right hand is placed first and highest on the shaft, with the thumb perpendicular.

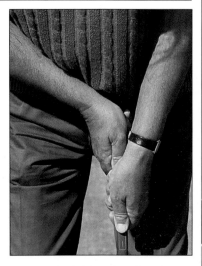

2. Then, the left hand is placed below the right, with the thumb also perpendicular. As always, the grip is light, with pressure coming mainly from the last three fingers of both hands.

THE PUTTING STANCE

Again, you will see many different putting stances, even at professional tournaments. Most players, however, favour a fairly narrow stance, with not more than 12 in (30 cm) between the feet, with the ball just inside a line that is level with the left instep.

This allows the putter to travel parallel to the ground or even slightly on the up at impact, thus getting the ball off to a smooth start. Striking the ball with the club face still on its downward path can make the ball bounce slightly on the surface of the green, causing you to lose control of distance and direction.

The feet, hips, shoulders and eyes should be parallel to the target line on all but the shortest putts, when the feet may be a little open (the left foot withdrawn slightly from the target line).

Many top-class players favour having more of the body's weight on the right foot, but that is because they can stand very still when putting, and they find it easier to line up if they have their weight more on the right foot (because this causes the head to be behind the ball). As most high-handicappers have great difficulty in remaining completely still during the stroke, they should try placing more weight on their left foot.

The putting stance

1. Narrow stance (12 in (30 cm) between feet). Hips, shoulders and eyes should be parallel to the target line. Knees slightly bent. Weight evenly divided between the heels and soles of your feet. Bend over from the waist so that your eyes are over and behind the ball.

2. This stance means that your chin is drawn in towards your body, enabling you to follow the line to the target with your eyes by simply swivelling your head, without in any way disturbing the stance that you have adopted.

THE PUTTING POSTURE

Keep your knees slightly bent and your weight evenly divided between the heels and soles of your feet. Bend forwards from the waist, so that your eyes are over and behind the ball and parallel with the ground. Your head is then bent over the ball, with your chin drawn in towards your body. You need only swivel your head to follow the line to the target.

Standing correctly

One of the most difficult positions to achieve is to stand the correct distance from the ball, so that when you bend forwards in the address position, your eyes are over the target line and behind the ball. Illustrated is the 'mirror trick', to help you get that all-important position correct.

Practising posture

Place a ball on a flat surface. Put a small mirror behind the ball and in direct line with the target. Now take your normal putting stance, with the putter behind the ball but not touching the mirror. Arrange your position so that you can see both eyes in the mirror. Your eyes are over the target line and slightly behind the ball.

Move away and then repeat a couple of times until you feel that you know when you are standing correctly to the ball. Then stand to the ball without the mirror, and when you feel that you are standing correctly, get someone to slip the mirror into place. If you can see your eyes in the mirror, then you have taken the correct position.

THE PUTTING MOVEMENT

The correct putting movement is a pendulum motion with the arms that removes all independent movement from the hands and wrists, everything moving backwards and forwards in one piece (the one-lever movement). The distance the ball travels is decided by grip pressure and length of backswing.

The degree of movement needed to move the ball a short distance is best judged and executed if you use your arms only and not your wrists and/or fingers. The design of the putter grip helps to eliminate unnecessary wrist/finger movement; and that is why the grip is different from that of all the other clubs.

For all but the short putt, the distance the putter head moves is the same on the backswing as on the follow through. Allow the club head to accelerate slightly on the forward swing. On the short putts, stopping the putter shortly after impact will give you a more distinct strike, helping to keep the ball on target.

The line of the backswing is slightly on the inside. The line of the downswing is from the inside and along the target line.

The forward press

A forward press will help you to start the backswing smoothly and on the correct path. This is done by 'pressing' your hands very slightly forwards towards the target in the instant before you commence the backswing.

Practising the putting movement

3. Swing the putter from the inside so that it passes through the original address position (the toe of the putter will then be as far from the shaft of the club on the ground as it was at the address position). In the photo, the ball has been struck and is on its way.

4. Allow the club to continue towards the target, with the blade facing the hole and the toe still the same distance from the shaft as it was when you addressed the ball. Stand completely still throughout.

   The correct path is: on the backswing, slightly on the inside; then back and through the address position and straight along the target line. (*Below*)

1. Arrange a club on the ground so that it is parallel with the target line. Put a ball beside the lower edge of the grip, allowing enough space between it and the grip to swing the putter comfortably. Address the ball.

2. After the forward press, swing back smoothly, slightly on the inside path. You will do this automatically if you avoid touching the thicker end of the grip on the ground. Should you touch the grip during the backswing, you have taken the putter back too straight or even on the outside. This makes it impossible to strike the ball correctly. (*Left*)

PRACTICE

Short putts up to 6 ft (1.8 m)

First, practise the short-putt swing without hitting any balls. Simply concentrate on making a smooth, short back-and-forward movement. Do this three or four times, or until you feel you have the right rhythm.

Next, take three balls and, without a target, strike them on the sweet spot, trying with each stroke to send the ball the same distance, *without* looking at the result of each stroke. Check then to see if the three balls have indeed rolled the same distance. If not, did you feel any difference when you struck the ball that didn't?

When you have been successful with this, repeat the exercise, this time with a slightly longer stroke.

This little starting session will, from the outset, help free your mind from the mechanics of the stroke. It will also help you to create the right feel for the movement and for the length achieved by that movement.

The putting routine

Repeat three or four times, to establish your putting routine, before choosing a hole that is level and only a short distance away, say 2 ft (60 cm). Go through the little routine you have just practised, that is, aim the putter at the target and take two practice swings without the ball to gauge the amount of movement your putter will need to roll the ball that far. Now place the putter head with the sweet spot centred on the ball. Only then do you position your feet so that the ball is inside a line to the left instep. Bend forwards so that your eyes are over the target line and just behind the ball. Check twice to see that the club face is pointed directly at the centre of the hole, then swing the arms back and forwards, striking the ball cleanly on the sweet spot.

Simply repeat the practice swing with which you satisfactorily gauged the distance to the hole. Above all, stand quite still throughout, especially at the finish of your stroke. Don't move your head to see

if the ball has gone into the cup. Keep your head still and *listen* to the satisfactory sound of it rattling in.

Do this with all three balls, going through the full putting routine each time. Then whenever you putt, either on the putting green or on the course, follow the same routine, which is an important aid to consistency.

Those who have not played a good deal previously may find putting practice tiring (even experienced players do), so a time limit of fifteen minutes is a good idea. This should enable you to play ten series of three balls per series before your concentration begins to fade. Remember that it is better to practise ten minutes a time, five times a week, than to practise once a week for fifty minutes.

Grade your progress

Write down the results of all putting drills – short, medium and long – so that you can pinpoint your weaknesses and concentrate on those drills that will help you to improve. Use a points system where

Practising the short putt

1. Choose a hole on a level surface and place three new balls of the same make 2 ft (60 cm) away and at 3, 6 and 9 o'clock from the target. Start with the 9 o'clock ball to avoid treading on the others.

possible – this will enable you to compare results and to move from success to success.

Practising the putting movement

In order to be able to strike the ball correctly, time after time, you must practise the putting movement to ensure that the

face points at the target at impact and the shape of the swing is correct from the start.

> **Evaluate your practice!**
> Always write down your results. Remember, if you get tired or start to lose your concentration, take a break before continuing.

2. Pick out an intermediate target, i.e. a mark of any kind over which you think the ball should roll in order to get it into the hole. Remove any loose impediments that are in the way.

3. Take two practice swings to create feel for the degree of movement you think necessary to get the ball into the hole.

4. Before taking your stance, place the putter behind the ball, so that the sweet spot and ball are in line with the intermediate target.

5. Check to make sure that the club face is pointing correctly at the intermediate target before you even consider starting the putting movement.

6. Concentrate your gaze on the back of the ball and, after a slight forward press, make your swing a copy of the practice swing that gave you the right feeling for the stroke. Strike the ball solidly. Stand still and listen. Do not move your head.

7. Repeat for the other two balls, each time using exactly the same routine from the very beginning. If successful, move a little further away, 3 ft (90 cm), and go through the complete exercise again using the same routine each time.

THE SHORT PUTTING GAME

It seems that the physically easiest part of the golf game, short putting, takes on so much importance that it becomes psychologically the most difficult. Certainly, all players, from the professional to the beginner, find that the shortest putts are sometimes impossible to sink consistently.

First, you must build up your confidence and this can only be done by experiencing success. Your routine will help you overcome nervousness due to doubt or fear. The use of an intermediate target to create a feeling of correct alignment is absolutely necessary; besides, it helps you to make a more decisive stroke. Without it, your putting stroke is likely to be tentative. A distinct strike from the sweet spot along a previously chosen line is the only way to continue sinking short putts. Line is more important than length with the short putts. The putt will hold its line if you stand still and strike the ball distinctly.

If for any reason you are disturbed when going through your putting routine, be sure to stop and start again from the beginning.

Drills for the short putt

3 x 3 balls:	strike and listen; check the distance achieved.
3 x 3 balls:	close your eyes and strike; again, check the distance achieved.
3 x 3 balls:	with another club lying on the ground to assist your swing path.
3 x 3 balls:	with only the left hand on the shaft, using only the arm.
3 x 3 balls:	with only the right hand on the shaft, using only the arm.

Putting drill for the short putts

This practice drill is excellent for learning how much backswing is needed to achieve a certain length. It also trains the ability to stand completely still while playing the short putts.

When you have done this successfully, stand further away from the tees and repeat, but this time change the order, starting with the tee furthest away and working back to the nearest.

1. Place three tees in the ground about 8 in (20 cm) apart and line up three balls about 18 in (45 cm) from the nearest tee.

Check the line and go through your usual pre-putting routine.

2. Strike the first ball, repeating your practice putt so that it stops at the first tee. Consider the length of backswing it took.

3. Same routine as always: strike the second ball to the second tee. How much longer was the backswing? Now strike the third ball to the third tee.

PRACTISING THE MEDIUM PUTT

When you have experienced success with your short putting, it is time to start on the medium putt, from 6 ft (2 m) to 20 ft (6 m). Start about 6 ft (2 m) away from the hole, using three balls. Now that you are further away from the hole, the pace, or speed, of the putt becomes increasingly important.

Furthermore, the correct use of your imagination is more necessary here – you have to learn to visualise the ball rolling along the chosen line and into the hole. To knock the ball into the hole, you must give it sufficient speed to reach the target and on the correct line. Should there be a slope, a ball approaching the hole from above has a theoretical chance of falling into the hole. A ball on the lower side, however, has no chance.

All putts are straight!

All putts are straight and the putted ball would continue in a straight line if the slope of the green did not cause it to curve from its original path. So you must choose the intermediate target with great care, so that when the ball has passed over it, the pace and curve of the green will take over and make the ball fall away on a curving line towards the hole.

Stand between the ball and the hole and check the pace of the green (the shorter the grass the longer the ball will roll). Is the hole uphill or downhill? Crouch behind the ball and check if the slope of the green is from left to right or right to left. The slope will have a greater influence on the ball the nearer it gets to the hole, because the ball is slowing down at that stage, and a slowly moving ball is more easily affected by the slope of the green. Once you have chosen the line, pick out an intermediate target, and take two practice swings, visualising the ball passing over the intermediate target, rolling along the line, and dropping into the hole.

If you didn't see a successful result, repeat until you do. Seeing the ball go into the hole when you take your practice swing will give you the confidence to repeat that practice swing when striking the ball. Eventually, this will put most of the mental responsibility on your practice swing, not on the actual putt, allowing you to play the putt in a more relaxed manner.

Only when you are satisfied with the imaginary result of your practice swings should you place the putter behind the first ball, preparatory to taking your stance. Be sure to place the sweet spot directly behind the centre of the ball and in line with the intermediate target. Check this twice

Practising the medium putt

1. Stand between the ball and the hole and study the distance between ball and cup, the pace of the green, and if it slopes uphill or downhill. Remove any loose impediments that are in the way.

before looking at the hole. Remember that it is imperative to stand at right angles to your intermediate target. Then, concentrating your gaze on the back of the ball, strike it, imitating your successful practice swing.

Study the result and, if unsuccessful, decide whether it was your mental picture of length and/or line that was at fault or if your putting stroke was incorrect. Then, making the changes you judge to be necessary, play the second ball from exactly the same position and with the same routine. If you miss once more, play the third ball, again taking into consideration the necessary changes.

Should the first ball be successful, pick another hole or move to a different spot, and start again.

This type of practice will help you decide whether it is the mental attitude or the actual stroke that needs to be improved.

2. Look at the hole from behind the ball and decide if it is level or slopes one way or the other. Only then can you choose a line and an intermediate target. Remember, it is better to exaggerate the line to the high side, because most medium-distance putts are missed on the low side.

3. Follow your by now established routine, taking the same number of practice swings as usual. Visualise the ball rolling along the line with sufficient speed to reach the target and fall into the hole.

4. Place the putter head behind the ball in line with the sweet spot and the intermediate target. Take your stance. Check your intermediate target twice before looking at the hole. Then concentrate your gaze on the back of the ball and strike it with a repeat of your practice swing. Stand still until the ball is well on its way.

THE MEDIUM PUTTING GAME

Good middle-distance putting depends on many things. First, the ability to judge the pace of the green (i.e., how fast or slow the green is on that particular day). Then you must be able to see the line on which you want the putt to roll. This takes practice and experience. Most middle-distance putts curve, so you can no longer aim directly at the hole. Instead, you have to aim to one side or the other. You must therefore choose a suitable intermediate target at which to aim. As far as you are concerned, the ball should be struck straight at the intermediate target and, of course, at the correct speed. Gravity then takes over, pulling the ball downwards and if you have aimed it at the correct intermediate target and at the correct speed, downwards and into the hole.

Correct practice and use of drills will improve your ability to imagine a successful result, thus increasing 'feel' for both length and touch. Be sure to decide first the pace of the green and then the line. (As a beginner, you would do best to exaggerate the amount you think the ball will curve, because courage does not come easily without experience.) The ball must be given enough speed to reach the target. Do not change your mind about the distance or direction during the playing of the stroke – just strike the ball as you have decided during your practice swings. Keep still until the ball is well on its way.

Remember, the key words for the medium putt are:
* pace
* line
* amount of movement

First, gauge the pace of the green, then choose your line, and, with a firmly established intermediate target in your mind, concentrate only on the length of the putting movement.

Drills for the medium putt

3 x 3 balls: usual routine. Strike and, without looking up, tell yourself immediately where the ball is in relation to the hole (e.g., short left, long right, centre short, in the hole).

3 x 3 balls: usual routine, but after set-up and alignment, look at the target while making the movement and striking the ball.

3 x 3 balls: usual routine. Strike the first ball just past the hole, the second ball just short, and the third the right distance.

These drills will enhance success considerably by increasing your ability to use imagination and by giving you that all-important 'feeling' for how long the ball will travel for the various lengths of swing.

LONG PUTTING

The idea behind long putting is somewhat different from that behind medium putting, although the object is the same. Given the difficulties involved (that hole looks very far away!), your attitude to the stroke is different. Here, you must try to get the ball near enough to the hole to allow an easy second putt. This means that you must move the ball the correct distance. A shift in emphasis has taken place: with the short putt, the line was most important; with the medium putt, line and length were equally important; but for the long-distance putt the length is paramount.

Advancing from success to success is the best way to learn to play better golf. Therefore, achieve success with the medium putt before going on to practise the long putt.

The pace of the green, the slope of the green, your grip pressure, and the length and speed of your backswing are the four paramount factors in long putting. Judging the necessary length correctly is extremely difficult. If you three-putt, it is nearly always the fault of the first attempt, that either sends the ball too far or too short. It is seldom that an incorrect line causes the extra stroke.

The idea is to imagine a circle around the hole where you want the ball to finish. The size and position of the circle (the hole does not always need to be in the middle) will depend entirely upon the length and difficulty of the putt.

Your routine is precisely the same as for the medium putt, but after choosing your intermediate target and taking your stance, your only interest should be in sending the ball the correct distance.

Practising the long putt

1. Place three balls close to each other, the same distance from the hole, say 15 yds (14 m).

2. Check the pace of the green from ball to hole. Remove any loose impediments that are in the way.

3. Examine the condition of the grass and the slope in the area of the hole, because this is where you want your ball to stop, leaving an easy second putt.

4. Go back to the ball and look from behind it at the line, choosing your intermediate target. Then start your established routine, concentrating on making smooth practice swings of the desired length and speed.

5. Before taking your stance, place the putter head behind the ball, which is to be in line with the sweet spot and the intermediate target. 'See' the ball rolling along the chosen line, stopping in the target circle you have chosen.

6. Concentrate your gaze on the back of the ball and strike it with a copy of your successful practice swing, thinking only of the distance you want to achieve. If successful with the first ball, change your target and start again.

THE LONG PUTTING GAME

Use your powers of observation as you walk towards the green and see which way it is sloping. If you find this difficult, try imagining that someone is pouring a bucket of water on to the green and see which way it flows. Once on the green, check its pace and the slope of the area around the cup, deciding where you want the first putt to finish. Choose your line, but remember to concentrate on the distance as this is the most difficult thing to judge with long putts. Imagine a circle around your target area: this will give you a bigger target to aim at, thus reducing tension.

A successful long putt is one of the most satisfying parts of golf and a stroke thus gained will send you to the next tee brimming with confidence.

Drills for the long putt

3 x 3 balls

First ball — No target, simply strike the ball and see how far it goes.

Second ball — Use established putting routine and strike the ball 2 ft (60 cm) past the first ball.

Third ball — Strike the third ball 2 ft (60 cm) past the second ball.

3 x 3 balls

Strike three balls from a marked spot on the practice green uphill towards a hole. Check the length of the backswing required to reach the target.

Gather in the balls and place them close together in the vicinity of the hole. Then strike the balls back down the slope to the marked spot. Check the length of the backswing now required.

3 x 3 balls

Make three concentric circles, say 2 ft (60 cm), 4 ft (120 cm) and 5 ft (150 cm) in radius around a hole on a flat surface. Place three balls about 40 ft (12 m) away. Play the balls as near as possible to the hole, giving yourself a points score, the highest for the smallest circle, and so on. Note the score for reference, when you practise again.

These drills are used to create a feeling for distances and for the amount of backswing and speed you require to attain them.

PUTTING FROM OFF THE GREEN

From time to time, you will find that even though your ball is not on the green it is better to putt the ball than risk a bad chip. If the grass between the ball and the green is not too long, the putter can be your best bet. Everything about the stroke is exactly the same as when on the green, with the following adjustments.

To avoid catching the longer grass between the club and the ball, put your weight more on the left foot, lean to the left, and have your hands well in front of the ball. This will create a downward strike that provides clean contact with the ball, sending it further than you would imagine, considering the longer grass between the ball and the green.

Don't be afraid of selecting the putter, even if the ball is lying badly – remember that a badly struck putt will cause less damage to your score than a bad chip.

Putting from off the green

1. The ball is on the foregreen, about 3 ft (1m) from the edge of the green, with a further 25 ft (8m) to the hole, which lies slightly downhill: a typical situation in which you should choose the putter, because with a lofted club you risk sending the ball too far.

2. Follow your usual putting routine, with those all-important practice swings to give you the right feeling for the swing required.

3. When addressing the ball, lean to the left, with the weight on your left foot and the hands well in front of the ball. Play the shot normally.

4. A satisfactory result: the ball finishes just past the hole, leaving an easy uphill putt. A shot has been saved, using common sense, imagination and your putter.

THE COMPLETE PUTTING GAME

Putting is that part of the game that is most variable. Sometimes, putts are missed for no apparent reason, causing loss of confidence and soaring scores. Do not allow this kind of situation to continue – something must be done.

Start by improving your reading of the green. For instance, it is worth noting that greens tend to lean away from high ground and towards the sea (if playing on a seaside course). Allow for slightly more slope than you think there actually is. The shorter the grass is cut, the longer the ball will roll and the more it will be affected by the slope; you must take this into account.

The nap of the green (the direction in

direction, it will be dull and dark (often called 'red') and the ball will stop much quicker. Therefore, you need a longer backswing to achieve the same distance.

Then create a putting routine that will be a constant factor in your putting game. As mentioned previously, routine will help you to concentrate, thus preventing your thoughts from leaving the job at hand and wandering – for instance, starting to worry about missing. Your routine will also create confidence, based on the feeling that you have made the right decision about line and the length of backswing. You must believe that what you are about to do will be successful.

Occasionally, it is impossible to find a suitable intermediate target, or you may even find one and lose it when standing to the ball. You must then use your imagination to help you stick to the decision that you have already made.

Strike the ball with the sweet spot, using the arms to create a smooth flowing movement, allowing the putter to move freely. Do not be over-mechanical or try to over-control the movement while making the stroke.

Make a habit of practising your putting routine: first, inspecting the pace and slope of the green before deciding on line and length, seeing always a successful result before taking up your stance. Then strike the ball immediately and with authority. Don't change your mind, and above all, stand still. Practise with a friend, competing with each other to create the atmosphere you will meet out on the course.

At some stage, if you have taken too many shots to reach the green, you may lose interest in finishing well, thus increasing your score even more. Remember that every shot has the same value. A good putt will put you in a more confident mood for the next hole.

Good putting seems to do something no other shot can do – it not only helps to keep your scores low, but it also makes the rest of the game a little easier and considerably more enjoyable.

You can't sink them all!

which the grass is cut and growing) will affect the speed of the ball. If the grass along which your ball will roll is cut away from you, it will be bright and shiny (green). The ball will roll faster and take longer to stop. Therefore, this putt needs less backswing.

If the grass has been cut in the other

CHAPTER THREE
GOLFING BASICS

The way you hold the club determines the position of the club head at impact, which in turn decides the direction, height and length of the shot. So don't regard your grip as simply a contact between you and the shaft of the club, because it is of primary importance to the result of the swing. How you hold the club is quite personal, due to the shape and size of your hands, so every golfer's swing is unique, despite the fact that all golf swings must attempt to do the same thing!

HOW TO HOLD THE CLUB

There are several different ways of holding the club, the most normal being the Vardon grip, also known as the overlapping grip, in which the little finger of the right hand overlaps the forefinger of the left. We illustrate three types of grip here.

Whatever grip you choose to use, remember that it should be firm and light, with most of the pressure coming from the last three fingers of the left hand and the middle two of the right.

With the hands in this position, they form a unit in which they work together. Should the V-shape between the respective forefingers and thumbs not be parallel, the hands will work independently, so the club face will be incorrect at impact. Remember:

* V-shapes parallel
* hands together
* firm but light and constant pressure from the last three fingers of the left and the two middle fingers of the right hand.

Holding the club too tightly will cause tension and greatly reduce the free flowing movement of the swing, causing crooked shots and lack of distance.

As your game improves and your swing grows stronger, you may need to change the position of your hands. However, as a beginner or high-handicapper, you should use the above hand positions. Adjustments may be necessary from time to time during your golfing career, either to re-discover that straight ball flight or to learn how to curve the ball in the air. If the hands are moved left on the shaft, the ball will tend to curve to the right, and vice versa. But all such changes to your grip should be discussed with your golf professional before you start to attempt them seriously.

The Harry Vardon grip

1. *The left hand first.* Be sure that the club head is placed correctly on the ground, with the club face square, pointing directly forwards. It should not be open (to the right) or closed (to the left). With your right hand at the top of the grip, hold the club steady so that the club face doesn't move off the target line. Now place the left hand so that it lies diagonally on the shaft from where the forefinger joins the palm to the underside of the pad at the base of your hand. Your left arm should be fairly straight.

2. With the right hand all the while keeping the club face still and pointing towards the target, fold the fingers of your left hand around the shaft, with the base of the left hand ¹/₂ in (1 cm) from the top of the club.

Lay the left thumb along the shaft. The natural curling of the fingers and the diagonal position of the hand will cause the thumb to lie slightly to the right of centre of the shaft. (*Right*)

3. Note how the thumb and forefinger of the left hand together create a line which points up towards the right shoulder. This means that you are holding the club properly with your left hand, and is a useful check whenever you are going through your grip routine, either on the practice range or when you are out on the golf course. (*Below left*)

4. Note that the end of the left thumb and the knuckle of the left forefinger are at the same height above the ground – also a useful routine check to ensure that you have the correct grip. (*Below right*)

Continued overleaf

The Harry Vardon grip, cont.

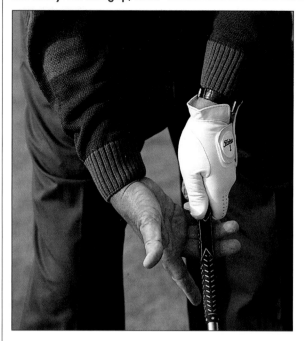

5. *Then the right hand.* With the right arm bent and elbow pointing towards the hip, place the right hand on the shaft slightly below the left, with the two middle fingers of the right hand under the shaft, as in the photo.

6. Curl the index finger of the right hand around the shaft and place your right thumb slightly on the left side of the shaft. Your left thumb should now be fitting snugly into the palm of your right hand.

7. Finally, place the little finger of your right hand over the knuckle of your left forefinger. As a beginner, you should always place the little finger of your right hand last, to avoid misplacing the right hand.

8. The hands are now correctly placed on the shaft with both lines between respective thumbs and forefingers pointing, parallel with each other, at the right shoulder.

The interlocking grip

This is used by players with shorter fingers who find it difficult to get the hands to function as a single unit.

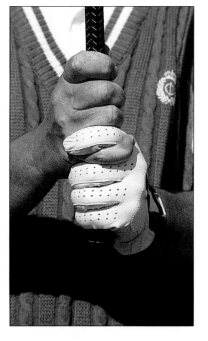

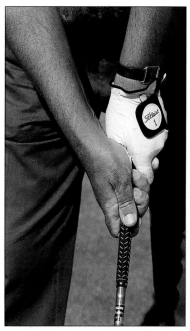

1. The little finger of the right hand is interlocked with the index finger of the left hand. Always place the little finger of the right hand in position last, otherwise there is a tendency to place the right hand too far to the right on the shaft.

2. The interlocking grip in the address position. Again, apart from the positioning of the fingers on the shaft, this grip is used in the same way as the Harry Vardon grip.

The two-handed grip

The two-handed (or full ten-finger) grip is often adopted by older players in an effort to increase the amount of wrist action and to create greater hingeing of the wrists.

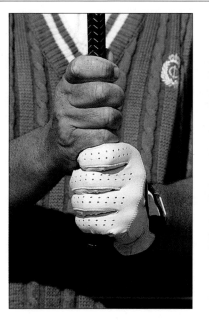

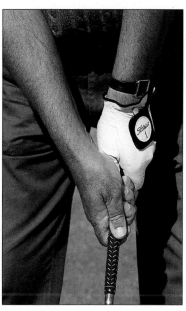

1. The positioning of the hands on the shaft.

2. The two-handed grip in the address position. Apart from the positioning of the fingers on the shaft, the grip is used in the same way as the Harry Vardon grip.

AIM

The high-handicap player spends a great deal of time concentrating on simply hitting the ball and not on aiming. Aiming the club properly usually comes as a later priority. But no matter how well you swing the club and hit the ball, your game will not improve if you do not aim correctly. The use of an intermediate target is a vitally important element in aiming well. You will remember that the concept of the intermediate target was also discussed in the previous chapter, when we were examining the question of putting.

The intermediate target

The intermediate target is any suitable spot within a couple of yards/metres of the ball over which you want the ball to fly (or roll if you are putting) in order for it to be on line to the target. It may be any kind of a mark – a leaf, a piece of discoloured grass, a divot mark – that you can see clearly and that you are quite sure is on the flight path of the ball to the target. Using the intermediate target as an integral part of your set-up and alignment drill must become an automatic element in your pre-shot routine.

In your pre-shot routine, always place the club head behind the ball with the

Intermediate target

1. Stand behind the ball and see in your mind's eye the flight of a successful shot. With this ball flight in mind, pick out a spot within a couple of club lengths of the ball, over which the ball must start if it is to take the planned route. This spot is your intermediate target and is all-important in helping you to aim the club correctly.

2. This discolouration in the grass will do fine as an intermediate target. If the ball flies straight over that, it should land just to the right of the flag on the high side of the green.

leading edge at right angles to a line running from the ball to the intermediate target. The two vertical lines of the face of the iron clubs will help you do this. Only then do you take your stance, first putting your right foot in position and then the left. Take care not to bring the club head out of alignment with the intermediate target. In other words, position the club first and then position yourself with reference to the club. Check that the club head is aligned with the intermediate target before looking towards the actual target.

Align your club head to the intermediate target every time you prepare to take a shot, so that it becomes an automatic part of your routine. This not only helps shot making but also makes it much easier to align feet and body.

The vast majority of golfers tend to aim first with the feet and then with the club face. This always results in the aim being far to the right of the target. The natural reaction to this is to try to change the swing path and the position of the club face in order to correct a faulty aim, thus complicating matters even further. Therefore, you must be sure that the club face is positioned correctly *before* you take your stance.

Target line

Picking the intermediate target, as just shown, is extremely important. However, it is also vital that you are aware of the target line, which runs in a straight line through the ball and the intermediate target.

1. Part of the target line is marked out here by a strip of white tape. It helps you to adopt the correct posture and stance. Eyeline, shoulders, knees and feet must be parallel to the target line.

2. The ball is struck first and then the tape and ground, taking a little divot. The club head then moves back inside the target line and up to the finish position. Being aware of the target line will also assist you to keep the club head on the proper swing path (*see* pp. 54 – 5).

When practising your aim, lay down a club 3 in (75 mm) outside the ball and pointing at the target. The two occasions when your club head is nearest to the shaft of the club on the ground should be at address and at impact. Another club can be laid in line with your toes, to ensure that you are standing parallel when playing the complete swing movement. Good aiming will assist you to swing the club towards the target and not only at the ball.

THE POSITION OF THE BALL

The position of the ball in the stance varies from individual to individual. Top professionals with magnificent hand and leg action favour a constant ball position, well forward in the stance (nearer the left foot). We mortals, however, need to vary the position of the ball to suit our level of prowess. On the opposite page, we give some guidelines.

STANCE

Adopting the correct stance is easier if you have aimed the club head correctly, using the intermediate target as a guide. When the club is properly aimed, the club face is pointing along the target line at the intermediate target. Then place your feet, first the right and then the left, so that they are at right angles to the target line. In other words, a line drawn from your left toe to your right toe would be parallel with the target line.

Because your swing should be shorter the nearer you are to the green, withdraw your left foot from the line to prevent slackness creeping into the swing movement and to allow each part of your body to move in the correct sequence during the swing.

Normally, the longer the swing you intend to take, the wider the distance between your feet and the more weight

Aim

No matter how well you swing your club, you won't achieve the desired result if you have not aimed properly. Correct aiming is a matter of high priority, and to achieve this you must use an intermediate target (*see* p. 46).

1. Place the club head behind the ball, so that the club face is pointing directly at the intermediate target.

2. Take your stance, making sure not to move the club head in relation to the intermediate target while you are arranging the position of your feet and body.

Practising the aim and stance
Place one club on the ground just on the far side of the ball, and another just in front of your feet. Both clubs should be parallel with the target line and when you stand to the ball, your eyes, shoulders, hips and feet should also be parallel to those clubs.

you have on your right foot when you address the ball.

Always follow the same routine: club head behind the ball and aimed correctly at the intermediate target; then the right foot in position, followed by the left.

For the complete swing movement, with the ball suitably placed, you will find that by 'softening' (holding it less tensely) and bending your right elbow, your right shoulder will be lower than your left. This will bring your head and upper body in the correct position behind the ball. Be sure, however, that your body alignment is still correct. Everything – that is feet, knees, hips, shoulders and (equally important) eyeline – should be parallel to the target line. You may turn your head slightly to the right, giving the impression you are looking at the back of the ball with your left eye, but the eyeline must not deviate from the parallel.

Stance

Experiment with various ball positions to establish the correct ones for your personal swing. A good rule of thumb is that when the club head is correctly placed and pointing at the intermediate target, the shaft should be pointing directly at your left groin.

So, place your club head behind the ball, aimed at the intermediate target, then position your feet, and finally check that the rest of your body is aligned properly.

For short irons – a centred ball. Place your feet so that the ball is centred between them. This gives the club head a steeper approach to the ball on the downswing and helps to give the shot height and back-spin. (*Right*)

For the medium/long irons – forward in the stance. Place your feet so that the ball is more forward in the stance (closer to your left foot). This gives the club head a more shallow approach to the ball, making the ball fly further.

For the woods from the tee – inside the left heel. Place your feet so that the ball is just inside the left heel. This causes you to strike the ball on the upswing, after the swing has reached the lowest point of its arc, producing a shot that starts on a low trajectory and results in maximum length.

The different ball positions can be seen easily here. The shorter irons require the ball to be nearer the feet and centred or slightly to the right of centre. As the shaft increases in length, the ball should be increasingly nearer the left foot. As the ball is already in position, you must position your body to the ball, not vice versa!

PRE-SHOT ROUTINE

We have already described pre-shot routine in the previous chapter, in which the art of putting was discussed. Pre-shot routine for all the other shots is basically the same – the most important aspect of your routine is that it is always the same! The key is that you are reminding yourself about all the vital elements of your golf shot: examining the lie of the ball, choosing the club, picking out the intermediate target, and playing your practice swings while seeing in your mind's eye a successful result of those practice swings. You are encouraging your mind to conjure up the feeling of coming to terms with the shot you are about to play – you have played this kind of shot well before and by going through the same pre-shot routine you are encouraging a repeat of that successful shot.

Follow your routine!
So, what you do prior to making your stroke and the order in which you do it is an essential part of your golf swing. All good players have a pattern or routine that they always follow.

First they look at the lie of the ball and then the target area, before they choose the club. Then they hold the club in the correct grip and pick out the intermediate target.

If the swing is a partial movement, they take a couple of practice swings, aiming at the target and imagining a successful flight and roll of the ball. Should it be a full swing movement, they take a 'mini-swing' to establish swing rhythm and get rid of unwanted tension in the arms. Only then is the club head placed behind the ball, with the club face pointing at the intermediate target.

The stance is taken, the right foot being positioned before the left. Then the feet are finally adjusted as the player checks his posture and alignment. The head swivels towards the target, imagining all the while the flight, bounce and roll of the ball,

terminating in a successful result. The head is not *turned* towards the target, as this could cause a change of shoulder position. Instead, it is *swivelled*, the right eye being lower than the left when looking along the target line.

The position of the club face is again checked, before the eyes are focussed on the back of the ball, but with the target still firmly in the mind's eye. The player then takes a constant number of waggles, and continues into the forward press which starts the backswing.

Some professionals even place the club behind the ball before taking their grip, but whatever you do be sure that your routine is always the same and should you be disturbed and lose your concentration, stop, and start again.

Important!
Although you are looking at the back of the ball, you should be seeing the ball flight in your mind's eye. This will encourage you to swing the club to the target and not only to the ball. Furthermore, your practice swings are a preparation for the swing to come and should be done at a similar speed as the actual swing. Purposeful, yes, but still leisurely. While your mind is thus engaged and relaxed by your usual routine, your concentration is sharp and remains on the job at hand, with no increase in your level of tension.

The pre-shot routine should move you smoothly into the start of the backswing with constant motion. Standing still over the ball will only cause increased tension.

Pre-shot routine _____

Your pre-shot routine has two goals: to put you in a confident frame of mind and to put your body in the correct stance, with good alignment every time. The series of photos shows practising from the fairway with the No. 9 iron and using a ball as the intermediate target.

1. First of all, one or two half swings to get the feeling of the club head 'freewheeling' through the hitting area. Always make the same number of practice swings.

2. The club head is placed behind the ball, aligned at the intermediate target.

3. The stance is then taken. Check the alignment of the club head to the intermediate target (has it changed since the previous step, when you aligned it?) and that the upper body is parallel to the target line.

POSTURE

Posture is the positioning of the body during the golf swing and is an element that the weekend golfer often neglects, to the detriment of his or her golf swing. In all good swings, the golfer leans forwards from the waist, with the shoulders relaxed and the arms hanging freely. This helps produce a free and unrestricted movement that makes for greater club-head speed and well struck shots of appreciable length. Any body tension during address is immediately reflected in loss of rhythm, which affects the strike and the length of the shot. Keep your back fairly straight and, with the longer clubs, the lower spine should be almost parallel to the line formed between the heels and the back of the knees. Good posture allows for a freer, more complete movement and reduces tension.

Because the right elbow is slightly bent and the right hand is below the left on the shaft, lower the right shoulder, otherwise the upper body would point far too much to the left, restricting your backswing.

For the longer shots the weight is predominantly on the balls of the feet and the greater the distance required, the more your weight should favour the right foot.

Flex the knees to assist good balance and weight transference, which will occur naturally during the swing if your set-up and alignment are correct. The right knee is inclined to the left in order to prevent the upper body from swaying. This puts weight on the inside of the right foot, enabling you to turn around the right hip.

The head and upper body are significantly behind the ball; they are increasingly further behind the longer the club you use.

Posture

The tee-shot posture is shown here. Note how the arms are hanging freely from the shoulders, with the hands inside the eyeline, and the body bent forwards from the waist.

The knees are slightly flexed and everything is parallel to the target line: feet, knees, hips, shoulders and – very important – the eyeline.

Note also how the right shoulder is lower than the left, and how the right elbow is bent and nearer the body than the left.

It is from this position that the backswing should move quite naturally into the correct path and plane.

FORWARD PRESS

Smoothness of swing movement is a prerequisite if you want to improve your golf – and who doesn't? – and nowhere is it more necessary and difficult than at the start of the backswing. If you start the backswing from a completely stationary hand position, there is a great danger of jerking the club head back from the ball, resulting in bad timing and often a radical change of the position of the club face at impact. The forward press will help you initiate the backswing smoothly on all your golf shots, including putting. When putting or playing short shots from around the green, the forward press is made by inclining the shaft forwards towards the target very slightly, a movement carried out only by the forearms immediately prior to starting the backswing.

With the longer shots, also move your right knee inwards towards the left, enabling the club to 'rebound' smoothly into the backswing.

N.B. When making the forward press, take care to do it gently so as not to touch the ball.

The forward press

The forward press leads to the start of the backswing and ensures that you don't jerk the club head away from the ball, but rather move it smoothly back.

The forward movement of the club rebounds softly into the backswing, so as to start the swing with a fluid motion.

1. The normal address position, with the hands over the ball and the shaft of the club pointing at the left groin.

2. The hands press forwards slightly until they are just in front of the ball, and the right knee moves forwards before rebounding smoothly into the backswing.

SWING PATH

A correct aim, stance, posture and mental picture of the desired flight will certainly encourage the correct swing path. The arms are swung back away from the ball and as the shoulders are pulled round by the arms, the club moves slightly to the inside and then up. So, the backswing line is *back-in-up*. On the way down, the arms are swung down with the club head approaching the ball from the inside of the target line, before swinging along the line at impact. (Not in-to-out and not out-to-in, but *down to the inside* and *along the target*

Swing path

I illustrate the path followed by the club head with the help of a thick length of black rubber that I have been using successfully for years.

The fact that one always stands to the side of the ball means that the club head can only be swung directly at the target for a very short part of the swing path. The club head moves not only back and up and down and forwards, but it also moves around the body, as illustrated.

1. The club head moves straight back from the ball and has already started to move inside.

2. It continues to move more to the inside at the same time as it begins to move up...

3. ...to a position in which the club shaft is parallel to the target line.

4. Then back down, somewhat more on the inside (compare this with photo 2).

line.) The follow through will then take the arms automatically to the inside and up to the finish. When your aim, stance and posture improve even more, and your swing becomes stronger, you will notice that the swing path up and down is not identical, but the club returns more from the inside due to the movement of the lower body.

Striking the ball from the inside will benefit both the line and length of your shot, because you can swing more freely from the inside, enabling you to allow the full use of the arms and the club, with the swing path pointing towards the target at impact.

5. Then along the target line just before and after impact. It is here that the club head is being swung directly at the target.

6. Moving once again to inside the target line and starting to move...

7. ...up, before continuing and...

8. ...moving round in plane.

SWING PLANE

The swing plane is the angle at which the arms and club are swung in relation to the ground. This angle is affected by your height, size, posture and the club that you are using. A long club will be swung flatter than a short club, because playing a short club will make you stand closer to the ball. Of course, tall, thin people tend to swing the club in a more upright plane than do short, corpulent players.

With the longer clubs, the club head must approach the ball from the inside of the target line so that, at impact, the club head is swung along the target line.

Therefore, the angle of the arms on the backswing should be as upright as possible, provided the club head is not allowed outside the target line.

There is a marked difference between the plane of the shoulders (they turn flatter) and that of the arms (they swing more upright), causing the stretching of the back and shoulder muscles and thus giving more freedom of movement, more power and more distance.

A correct plane will benefit your swing greatly and will produce proper shot trajectory, whatever the club chosen.

CLUB-HEAD SPEED

If your maximum club-head speed is to be reached and maintained at impact, a smooth swing *through* the ball to the finish position is essential. Don't swing *at* the ball, swing *through* it to a full, balanced follow-through position. A light grip and a tension-free position at address, combined with an easy forward press, will allow you to swing the club smoothly back from the ball. Remember that the club has to change direction at the top of the back-swing, and a smooth change of direction will be spoiled if the backswing is rushed.

Swing the club back using the left hand and arm (the right hand and arm do not exert themselves) and the result will be a smooth, controlled backswing. 'Smooth' is the word to remember throughout the swing.

When you swing the club down, the shaft will arch forwards slightly, leaving the club head trailing. The shaft straightens out at impact and this occurs only if you allow your hands, arms and club freedom of movement.

A full, smooth, balanced follow through and full freedom from tension are what counts here, not brute strength. In the beginning of your golfing career, you will find that a well-struck shot with a full swing movement at three-quarter speed will always send the ball further than if you try to knock it out of sight. Correct club-head speed and swing tempo will give you better control and balance, thus improving your club-head–ball contact. It is only the correct striking of the ball and the club-head speed that determines distance.

WARMING UP

Before starting a practice session or a round of golf, be sure to warm up properly. This will prevent you from straining muscles and will improve your early shots, either on the practice ground or on the course. Too many rounds of golf are spoiled by bad first and second holes

caused by cold, unelastic muscles. The exercises opposite will prepare you for practising or playing, and will make you supple and free from stiffness. First of all, loosen up by various stretching exercises and by swinging your arms freely. Then follow the exercises opposite.

1. Place a club behind your back in the crick of the elbows and turn the shoulders back and forth without moving your feet. Repeat twenty times.

2. Using your left hand only, swing with the club upside down, holding it by the shaft, not by the club head. The left arm should do all the work and the club shaft should make a whistling sound as it swings through the air.

3. Then start swinging a club with your feet together. The first two or three swings should be very short; then allow the swing to develop into a half swing, then a three-quarter swing.

4. Finish with ten full swings.

5. Ten full swings again, but this time holding three clubs together.

6. Last of all, take some swings from a left-handed position (if you are a right-hander). Swinging the club left-handed helps loosen the muscles that you use in the backswing (when playing from the normal right-handed position).

CHAPTER FOUR
CHIPPING

In the chip-and-run shot the ball spends the minimum amount of time in the air and the maximum amount of time on the ground. The shot is used to play a ball from the foregreen or the fairway on to the green and close to the hole. The shot to play and the club to choose are dictated by the lie of the ball and the fact that the intervening ground is unsuitable for the use of the putter.

The chip-and-run shot with the right club will get the ball into the air at the correct height, fly it over the foregreen, land it gently on the front edge of the green, and roll it to the flag. The stance and posture will help to create a descending blow, causing the ball to roll up the club face and producing the required height without the use of the hands or wrists.

THE SHORT CHIP-AND-RUN SHOT

The short chip-and-run shot is, like the putting stroke, a one-lever movement. If played correctly, it gives great accuracy.

The two-lever movement (arms and wrists) is used when greater height and length are required. This movement is described later in this chapter, where we cover the long chip-and-run.

The choice of club

The club you need to make this shot can vary from a No. 4 iron to a sand iron. The correct choice will depend on the following factors.

1 *The lie of the ball.* Is it a good lie (sitting neatly on top of the grass), is it lying on hard, bare ground, or is it nestling in the grass of the semi-rough?

2 *The distance to the edge of the green.* Always allow for a safety margin, so that a shot struck with less than 100% will still carry the intervening ground and land on the putting surface.

3 *The distance from the landing point to the flag, and the condition and slope of the green.* The example opposite will make it easier to understand. The ball is about 3 ft (1 m) from the edge of the green, which slopes away from you and is medium-paced. The flag is 33 ft (10 m) from the edge. The ball is lying well, but there is some longer grass between it and the green, preventing you from using the safest club, the putter.

You want the ball to clear the uncut grass on a low trajectory to land about 6 ft (2 m) into the green. In other words, it must fly 9 ft (3 m) before bouncing a couple of times and rolling the remaining 27 ft (8 m) to the flag. As the flag is down the slope, you should try to get the ball to stop slightly past the hole, as an uphill putt is easier.

You know from previous experience that a No. 7 or 8 iron should do the job, *if* you use a movement similar to that for the long putt.

As far as the movement is concerned, the normal chip-and-run shot reminds us of the putting stroke, the only difference being that the ball leaves the ground because the irons are built differently than the putter. On the club face there are a number of grooves, two vertical and eight to ten horizontal. The vertical grooves help you to aim the club, while the horizontal ones create back-spin and control.

The angle of the iron club's shaft to its head is flatter, so you must stand a little further away from the ball than you would if you were using the putter. For shots of this type, hold the club further down the shaft with your normal grip (for instance, the Vardon grip), because the grip on the iron club is round, not flattened like the putter.

The No. 7 iron has approximately a 35° loft, so to strike the ball correctly hit it at its base and just before the club head has reached its lowest point (just before making contact with the grass). The same amount of movement with a No. 4 iron would send the ball on a lower trajectory and roll it past the flag; with a No. 9 iron or a wedge, the ball would have increased height but would pull up and stop before getting close to the flag.

This means that you have to create a picture of the ball's flight and roll in your mind's eye *before* you choose your club.

The chip-and-run grip

Holding the club correctly and aiming the club head towards the intermediate target are probably the least exciting parts of golf, but they are absolutely the most important. If you don't hold the club correctly, aim it correctly and stand correctly to the ball, your chances of a successful shot are very slight indeed.

We have shown already the standard golfing grip in detail (pp. 22 – 3) and this is the grip that is used for the chip-and-run shot, *except* that the hands are further down the shaft, giving you greater control.

The chip-and-run

1. The ball is lying well on top of the grass, 3 ft (1 m) from the edge of the green, and there is a further 33 ft (10 m) to the flag.

2. Choose your intermediate target and visualise the trajectory, the landing spot, the bounce and the roll of the ball towards the flag.

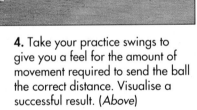

3. Hold the club further down the grip than normal. Open the stance slightly, with most of your weight on the left foot. Note the triangle formed by arms and shoulder line. (*Left*)

4. Take your practice swings to give you a feel for the amount of movement required to send the ball the correct distance. Visualise a successful result. (*Above*)

5. Address the ball and repeat your practice swing in 'reality', striking the ball with a crisp pendulum movement.

6. The follow through is the same length as, but slightly lower than, the backswing. The triangle remains the same throughout.

Stance

Place the club head on the ground, flat on its sole and with the club face aimed at the intermediate target. Be sure that the shaft is straight (your hands neither in front of nor behind the ball). Then take your stance in the following way.

1 With your feet the same distance apart as for the putt, keep your knees flexed, the toes of both feet swivelled very slightly to your left and your weight mainly on the left foot. Move your arms, hands and shaft so that they are in front of the ball and ensure that you have a straight line from your left shoulder through your left arm and shaft to the club head. Check to see that the club face still points towards the intermediate target.

2 Now open the stance a little by moving the left foot back 3 – 4 in (8 – 10 cm). This turns the lower part of your body slightly towards the target; this, together with the flexed knees and the weight on the left foot, helps to ensure a downward blow that strikes the ball first and then the grass, creating the desired trajectory.

Important!

When you open the stance, only the *lower* part of the body (feet, knees and hips) should be turned slightly towards the target, *absolutely not* your chest, shoulders and eyeline. These must remain parallel to the target line. Otherwise, you will not be aiming the shot correctly.

Posture

With knees flexed and pointing a little towards the target, weight on the left foot and with a shortened grip, the hands should be in front of the left thigh and just above the knee.

Those parts of the body nearest the target (left arm, hip and shoulder and the left side of the face) should be in front of the ball, which is centred between the feet.

The beginner will find this position tiring, so don't practise it for too long.

Every few minutes, stand up straight, stretch and rest a little.

When you have adopted the correct posture, the left arm and the club shaft will form one side of a triangle. The other side is formed by the right forearm, and the third by a line between the shoulders. This triangle should remain constant throughout the movement.

Movement

The movement is similar to that of putting, with the *arms only* creating the necessary amount of back-and-forward motion, and no wrist movement for the shorter chips. The distance the club head travels dictates the length the ball will fly and is the same on the backswing and on the follow through. This is sometimes difficult to see, as the club head on the follow through should finish closer to the ground than it was at the top of the backswing. This is due to the weight being mainly on the left foot.

Practise creating the pendulum movement with natural acceleration down to the ball, holding the finish position with the triangle intact and the club face pointing towards the target, ensuring that the weight is constant on the left foot and that the movement comes only from the arms.

With the experience gained from practising the chip-and-run, you will understand how the choice of club, the address position and backswing will affect the length and height of the shot, and the amount of roll after landing.

The chipping swing movement

1. The arms only create the swing, which is a pendulum movement. Shown here is the backswing. (*Above*)

2. On the follow through, the club head travels as much forwards as it did on the backswing – a true pendulum movement. (*Below*)

PRACTISING THE SHORT CHIP-AND-RUN SHOT

We show here an excellent way of practising your short chip-and-run shot, using tees to help you ensure that the ball is struck first (with a descending blow), thus creating the height necessary to land the ball just on the green and roll it up to the flag. Practising like this also helps you to understand the importance of keeping the triangle formed by the arms and shoulder line intact throughout the movement.

When you have practised in this way and you are satisfied with the success you have achieved, take a rest before changing the club and the target. Do not use any tees this time, but go through the illustrated routine once more, striking the ball first and the grass afterwards, keeping your triangle intact.

When you feel that you have mastered this, the next phase in your step-by-step approach to successful chipping is playing the same shot from the same position and to the same target but with different clubs, to gauge the difference in the results obtained and to gain experience of the trajectory and length of roll of each club. In other words, you must learn how far each club will fly the ball and how far the ball will roll after landing, given that you strike the ball with exactly the same movement.

Do not neglect practice from sloping positions too. A downhill lie requires a more lofted club, and vice versa. Side-slope shots should also be practised; you will find your practice swings immensely helpful in determining the point of contact between club and ground, and the direction the ball takes.

Practising the short chip and run _____

Drills for the short chip-and-run

3 x 3 balls
All balls to be the same distance from the edge of the green. First three from a good lie. Next three from a mediocre lie with a more lofted club. Last three from a bad lie and with an even more lofted club. Repeat the last three using the putter. Compare the results. Would it have been better to use the putter in this situation? (*See* page 36.)

You will see that the worse the lie, the more lofted the club should be.

3 x 3 balls Uphill lie
Use a club with *less* loft than you would choose if on an even lie.

3 x 3 balls Downhill lie
Use a club with *more* loft than you would choose if on an even lie.

3 x 3 balls
Play on to an upward-sloping green using a *less* lofted club.

3 x 3 balls
Play on to a downward-sloping green using a *more* lofted club.

3 x 3 balls Side-hill lies
Take extra care with your practice swings to determine where the club comes into contact with the ground. Note that if the ball is higher than your feet, it tends to go left of target, and vice versa.

1. Tee up about six balls and with a No. 8 iron play them at a specific target. Make sure that you strike the ball with a descending blow and that you make contact with the tee, knocking it over.

2. When you have been successful in striking both ball and tee every time, play them again, but this time with the tees lying on the ground about 2 in (5 cm) in front of the balls.

3. Striking the ball first and the tee afterwards is proof that you have struck the ball with a descending blow. Remember to think as well of the length of shot you want to play – all your successful shots should end up in the target area.

4. Only when you have gone through these steps successfully should you move on to practising the chip without a peg. Play the ball from the grass and remember to strike the ball first and then the grass. Never try to scoop the ball up in the air, just let the loft of the club do its work and the ball will lift correctly.

THE LONG CHIP-AND-RUN SHOT

When you are some 30 – 40 yds/m from the front edge of a long green with the flag well at the back, or if the green is double-tiered, your best bet could well be a long chip shot. The ball should fly fairly low, land well on the green and roll up to the flag. A high-trajectory ball flight is not only more difficult to judge when playing into a long green, but is more difficult to execute than the simple chip.

The choice of club

Even if the ball has a perfect lie, experience is the only thing that will help you here, as the distance to the green, compared to the distance to the flag, must be considered. A No. 8 or a No. 9 iron could be correct considering the distance the ball must travel in the air, compared to the distance it must cover on the ground.

Grip

Place your hands on the shaft as for the short chip-and-run shot, but higher up on the grip, because more movement is now needed to create the added distance required. About 1 1/2 in (4 cm) from the top is usually sufficient.

Stance

Take your stance only after you have visualised the shot and then seen a successful result with your practice swings. As always, the routine should be the same, the club placed behind the ball first, with the club face pointing directly at the intermediate target before you take your stance. As the distance you want the ball to travel increases, so does the distance between your feet. Keep your stance slightly open, with the weight favouring the left foot and more towards the balls of the feet. The ball should be back in the stance and the left arm and club shaft should be in a straight line.

Remember that it is only the lower part of the body that is open (turned to the left), not the shoulders or eyeline; otherwise the ball will very likely follow the shoulder line and finish considerably to the left of the target.

The long chip-and-run shot

1. The ball is lying well some 30 yds/m from the front edge of the green and the flag some 55 yds/m away.

2. Take a practice swing without the club, visualising the trajectory and length required for a successful shot. This helps you pick the right club for the shot, in this case a No. 9 iron.

3. Follow your normal pre-shot routine, feeling how the lengthened practice swing causes weight transference and a change of knee position.

4. Then play the ball in exactly the same way as your successful practice swings, which gave you the right feeling for the length of shot required.

5. When you have played your shot, hold the finish position and watch the result. This aids feedback, which increases your understanding that length of swing and choice of club affect both the length and trajectory of the shot.

Posture

The head should be over the ball and the hands well in front of it. Flex the knees because the increased movement on the backswing will cause a slight weight transference from left to right on the backswing and from right to left (but more so) on the downswing.

Movement

Although the swing is taken with the arms, the weight of the club head may cause the wrists to break slightly if the backswing is long enough. But the long chip is primarily an arm swing, distinct and robust, sending the ball fairly low before it lands on the putting surface, its trajectory and forward momentum sending it after two or three bounces rolling up to the flag. The amount of forward swing encourages the knees to follow, so that even more weight is on the left foot at the finish of the swing than at the address, and your right heel is slightly raised at the finish position.

PRACTISING THE LONG CHIP-AND-RUN SHOT

This type of shot is often called for during a round of golf, so your game will benefit if you practise it regularly. For some reason, many golfers consider this an easy shot, so their concentration is not always as sharp as it should be, resulting in poor visualisation and a lack of success. When they have a difficult chip to play, they concentrate more, and their improved visualisation as a rule leaves the ball only 2 or 3 yds/m from the flag. But the normal long chip-and-run shot, easy as it seems to execute, needs the same sharpness, otherwise you will find yourself too far from the flag to have a reasonable chance of finishing off with a single putt.

Therefore, always use your imagination before choosing the club and type of shot to be played. Use the same pre-shot routine as always; seeing a successful result with your practice swing is a must.

Vary the lie of the ball, not forgetting uphill and downhill shots. Compete with yourself and see how many times out of ten the ball lands in the chosen area and how many times it rolls the correct distance. Vary your choice of club and swing length in order to create feedback. Remember this is the golf swing in miniature. The correct execution of this shot will enhance your chances of swinging the club correctly when you come to use the half, three-quarter and full swing movements.

Practising the two-levered chip

Taking about ten balls on to the practice ground, pick a suitable target area where you want the ball to land if you play it with your No. 9 iron. In this example, the area is about 25 yds (23 m) away.

1. Take your practice swings to gauge the length of swing required to play the ball 25 yds (23 m).

2. The address position with the No. 9 iron: ball in the centre of the stance, weight favouring the left side, and hands just in front of the ball. Light grip pressure.

3. On the backswing, the wrists cock slightly due to the light grip and the length of the swing.

4. The ball is struck and on its way. Note how the triangle formed by the arms and shoulder line is maintained all the way.

5. Hold the follow-through position to get feedback concerning the length of swing you used to achieve this shot length. Note how this photo is a perfect copy of the practice swing in photo 1, opposite, except that the ball is well on its way to the target area.

THE RUN-UP SHOT

The run-up shot is used when there is not enough room between the front edge of the green and the flag to land the ball and stop it before it rolls well past the flag. The choice of club is usually one with little loft, which sends the ball low so that it rolls sufficiently after bouncing on the foregreen to reach the green and stop near the flag. You can also use it if you have landed to the side of the green and there is a bank between the ball and the green, with insufficient room to land the ball on the green and stop it before it rolls too far. Grip, stance and posture are the same as for the chip shot, but the ball is played further back in the stance in order to keep it low and run it up the bank and on to the green.

If you are not sure of yourself when it comes to this kind of shot, you are in danger of changing the club speed during the stroke. Once you have made up your mind, play the shot exactly as you did your successful practice swing. Keep your eye on the back of the ball throughout the swing and keep the head still until well after the ball has been struck. Remember, too, that it is better to be past the flag and on the green, rather than just short of the green and on the fringe.

THE CHIPPING GAME

The secret of good chipping is the ability to 'see and feel' the shot before you make it. This helps you to choose the right club, the right landing spot, and the right amount of backswing.

In all chip shots the body is fairly stationary and only the arms are used, making for a decisive shot. The chip can be used from the very edge of the green up to a distance of 55 – 65 yds (50 – 60 m) out, depending on your choice of club and the length of your backswing. The movement is one-lever for the short chips and switches to a two-lever movement when the backswing is long enough to make the wrists cock naturally. Longer chip shots are played in the same way, with an open stance but with the hands a little higher up on the shaft; also, with a more lofted club and longer backswing to achieve the increased height and length desired.

When making the longer backswing, the swing will automatically change to a slight two-lever movement because the weight of the club head moving back through a longer arc causes the wrists to break slightly. This makes it more difficult to return the club face to exactly the same position that it had at address, so you must avoid excessive wrist movement, retaining the triangle and keeping the club head low to the ground on the follow through. Returning the club face correctly to the address position is one of the most important elements of the successful golf swing, be it a long chip, a half swing or a full-blooded drive.

If in doubt when choosing between, say, a No. 7 or a No. 8 iron, pick the club with the most loft, because having your hands in front of the ball will de-loft the club slightly. A club with not enough loft encourages you to try to scoop the ball into the air – with disastrous results.

Chipping has one thing in common with the long putt – it is more difficult to achieve the correct length than the correct line, so practice swings are vital.

As is the case of all shots from around the green, it is here that even the most inexperienced players can cut their scores, by using common sense and imagination, with the confidence to repeat exactly what they believe to be a suitable practice swing.

The run-up shot

Illustrated is a typical situation in which the run-up shot should be considered. The ball has missed the green to the right by some 18 ft (6 m). The ground slopes upwards towards the green and there is insufficient room between the edge of the green and the flag to chip or even pitch the ball and have it stop anywhere near the flag, as the green itself slopes downwards towards the flag. The solution is to run the ball up the slope with enough speed to reach the green and then roll downhill towards the flag.

Of great importance to a successful result is the pre-shot routine, seeing in the mind's eye the successful results of the practice swings, with the ball bouncing and then rolling up the bank before rolling on to the green and finishing by the flag. The actual shot must be an exact copy of the successful practice swing.

1. The ball is to the side of the green, lying well. There is very little room between the edge of the green and the flag, making necessary the use of the run-up shot.

2. The choice of club for this particular shot is the No. 5 iron. Shorten your grip and hold the club firmer than usual. The ball should be played well back in the stance (towards your right foot). Take your practice swings and, as usual, visualise the perfect result. Remember that it is better that the ball travels too far, as it must roll on to the green and not fasten in the fringe. A long putt back is usually easier than another chip.

3. The ball is struck with a downward blow and is on its way. Hold the follow-through position, as the ball bounces up the slope and on to the green, then rolls to the flag.

CHAPTER
FIVE
PITCHING

The pitch shot is the shot that you play on to the green from various distances when you need the maximum amount of air time and the minimum amount of ground time; for instance, when you want to lift the ball over a greenside bunker and to make it stop quickly after landing. In this respect, it is the opposite of the chip-and-run shot. There are three ways of making the ball stop quickly: by giving it back-spin, by giving it a high trajectory, or by playing it slowly so that it lands softly.

The choice of club for the pitch shot is usually between the pitching wedge and the sand iron, the most lofted clubs in the bag; these will both produce maximum height. The beginner will find the pitching wedge less 'dangerous' to use since the leading edge on the pitching wedge is lower than that on the sand iron. Stick to the wedge until you are proficient.

When you strike the ball correctly with the pitching wedge (that is, with a downward blow, striking first the base of the ball and then the grass), the club's sharp leading edge will, together with its loft, give the ball back-spin and cause it to rise quickly and steeply.

THE SHORT PITCH

The short pitch is played when the ball is not required to travel too far or too high (for instance, when you must play over a greenside bunker), but when it has to stop fairly quickly to finish near the flag.

Grip
Hold the club in the usual way, but 2 – 3 in (5 – 8 cm) lower down on the shaft and slightly firmer than normal to encourage a decisive downward strike.

Stance
The feet are close together in an open stance and the knees are slightly bent. The ball is positioned in the centre of the stance.

Posture
Keep your weight predominantly on the left foot, the hands just in front of the ball, and the head and upper body behind the ball.

Short pitch over a bunker

1. Examine the lie of the ball and the distance between a safe landing spot and the flag. See in your mind's eye the ball fly over the bunker, land at the chosen spot and stop by the flag.

2. Before playing the shot, be sure to look at the landing area, *not* into the bunker! Now repeat that successful practice swing, taking the club back from the ball in exactly the same way and letting your left arm lead the club back to the ball.

3. With intermediate target chosen and practice swings taken, place the club head behind the ball before taking your stance. Always the same routine: club head first and then the stance.

4. The ball is struck and safely on its way, slightly upward (to the left) of the flag, which is on a downward-sloping green.

5. Hold the finish position, with left arm and club in a straight line and club head low to the ground. Keep still until the ball has stopped – this gives you feedback.

Movement

The short pitch is a double-lever movement. Use your arms to swing the club back and then break early with your wrists to swing it up. Swing the club down through exactly the same position you had at address, hands slightly in front of the ball, holding the club firmly. Stop the club soon after the strike, with the left arm and the club shaft in a straight line, pointing at the flag, with the club head close to the ground. This helps to create sound contact and back-spin.

PRACTISING THE SHORT PITCH SHOT

Confidence is of primary importance in this situation. If you are not confident, the danger is that you will change your mind while actually making the stroke and the swing will lose its rhythm. Intelligent practice with this type of shot is essential to build up confidence; this can only be done by proper step-by-step practice from the very outset.

Each practice session should consist of three series of ten shots each. To ensure success from the very start, place the first series of ten balls on a medium-low tee. You will see that when you strike the tee with a downward movement of the club head, the ball will lift enough to clear an intervening bunker. All you have to do to change the trajectory of the ball is to alter the steepness of the backswing.

When you are happy with the first series of ten, go on to the second series, this time without teeing up the balls. When you have finished this series satisfactorily, take a break before going on to the final series, which you also play without tees.

The short pitching game

The short pitch is a very useful shot to master. It is not only a stroke-saver but it also improves your ability to imagine successful results; success, as we have already said, breeds confidence.

It is absolutely impossible to reach the green every time in the regulation number of shots – even for a professional playing at his best. Incorrect club choice, weather conditions, bad bounces or indifferent striking will cause the ball to miss the putting surface some time or other during the game. This, together with modern course architecture (greens tend to be more 'protected'), will often leave you with a short pitch to play, usually over a mound or a bunker. So it is very important that you learn to approach this situation with confidence. The ability to play short pitches well will put less pressure on the rest of your game.

Remember, strike the ball first and the ground afterwards. The more height required, the earlier the break of the wrists, making the swing narrower and steeper. If you use the arms only and don't break the wrists, the swing movement will be backwards and forwards on a low arc; this will produce too low a flight. When you bring the wrists into play, the swing becomes steeper and produces the required increase in height.

THE NORMAL PITCH SHOT

This is the shot played with the wedge from distances up to 90 yds (85 m) from the flag. You may be able to hit the ball further with your wedge, but it is inadvisable, since this club is for precision shots. Your aim is not just to land the ball on the green; you want it to finish near the flag. Leave the longer wedge shots to the professionals.

Grip

The grip is the usual one, but with the hands about $1\frac{1}{2}$ in (40 mm) down the shaft to give the necessary control.

Stance

Stand with the feet about 15 in (40 cm) apart and the left foot slightly open (pointing slightly towards the target). In other words, the left foot is withdrawn about 3 in (75 mm) from the target line. The ball is centred in the stance.

Posture

Centre your weight on the balls of the feet. Let the arms hang loosely from the shoulders, with the left arm and the club shaft in line, which means that the hands are in front of the ball. Take care that, with the open stance, it is only the feet, knees and hips that point to the left and not the shoulders. Shoulder, chest and eyeline must be parallel to the target line, otherwise the ball is likely to fly to the left.

The normal pitch

1. Go through your normal pre-shot routine (practice swings, imagining the successful result, etc.) before addressing the ball, using the intermediate target to ensure proper alignment. *(Right)*

2. The length of the backswing is dictated by the distance required and its steepness by the height required. With a longer backswing, your weight will be transferred to the inside of the right foot.

3. The ball is struck and on its way. The left hip has cleared to the left and the arms continue up and around. The head is still, not yet following the swing.

4. Because the follow through is as long as the backswing was, your weight transfers to the left foot and the head now starts to move around.

5. The finish position: weight more on left foot, only the toe of the right foot is in contact with the ground, the hips are facing the target and the eyes are following the path of the ball. The successful shot provides you with a positive information feedback, which will increase your confidence.

Movement

The forward press starts the club on the backswing with the wrists bending early in the movement, causing the club head to swing up in a narrow arc. The movement causes the weight to transfer to the inside of the right foot, with the left heel remaining on the ground, even though the shoulders have been pulled round 70 – 80°. On the downswing, the left arm pulls the club head down on the inside of the target line, and the left side accompanies the left arm as it passes through the hitting area and pulls the upper body through to the finish position, which must be in perfect balance.

The leg movement complements the arm swing, the open stance restricting leg and lower body movement on the backswing while allowing the shoulders to turn. On the downswing, the open stance encourages the movement of the legs, helping to keep everything in correct sequence and therefore returning the club head to its original position at impact.

THE NORMAL PITCHING GAME

The successful normal pitch is a stroke-saver for golfers at all levels, enabling you to land the ball near the flag with a possible one-putt finish. For the beginner, a successful normal pitch will at least never miss the green.

The shot itself is the first example of the normal swing, with weight transference to the right foot on the backswing. The amount of backswing is less than the full swing movement, making it necessary to have the stance slightly open, which ensures that no slackness creeps into the movement and keeps every part of the movement in its correct chronological sequence.

When you use the short-shafted, heavy-headed wedge, it is all too easy to force or rush the shot, which tends to close the club face and change the swing line, often sending the ball long and to the left. The open stance helps create tautness in the backswing and encourages left-side dominance, thus ensuring that your ball never starts to the left.

PRACTISING THE NORMAL PITCH

First, be sure that the distance you want to achieve doesn't necessitate your having to hit the ball hard, thereby causing a loss of precision. Create good rhythm and timing by taking a sufficient number of practice swings, all the time imagining the successful flight and bounce of the ball.

Play ten or twelve balls at a time at the same target, being sure to go through your normal pre-swing routine before every shot.

When you have succeeded in landing most of the balls in the same area, experiment by changing the ball's position in your stance and by altering the steepness of the backswing, in order to see how your ball trajectory changes. However, be sure to allow the loft of the club to create the height, always striking the ball first and the ground afterwards. Never try to scoop the ball into the air.

Create feedback by comparing the length and steepness of your swing with the length and height of the ball flight. This will give you valuable experience which you can use to advantage when playing out on the course. This will also teach you the necessary feeling for this shot.

Every practice session, no matter what club you are using, should be concluded with a series of pitch shots, leaving you with a feeling of success before putting your clubs away.

Pitching drills

To enhance control and accuracy when pitching, here are a couple of drills you can do.

1. With the feet together. The degree of upper body movement and swing speed is restricted when playing shots with the feet together. Therefore, the length of the backswing is paramount in creating sufficient movement to send the ball the required distance.

2. The follow through continues to a position that is similar to the backswing, which means that this movement is akin to a pendulum movement – as long on the follow through as it is on the backswing.

3. A very effective drill is to make the pitching movement and let go with your right hand after impact. Sounds strange, but it really does help the left arm to learn how to swing the club so that it pulls the body through to a controlled and well-balanced finish position.

THE HIGH, SOFT PITCH

Playing a high, soft pitch is your only choice when left with some 30 or 40 yds/m from a good lie to a flag that is just behind a bunker or near the front edge of the green. The chip-and-run and the normal pitch would be unsuitable, as the ball would fly too far or would not stop quickly enough. What is needed is a slow, high shot that will land softly and steeply on the green.

The experienced player has a choice of club here: the pitching wedge or the sand iron. If the lie is very good (sitting up on the grass) and the landing area is small, the sand iron gives you the best chance of success, because it will fly the ball higher and stop it quicker. Less experienced players, however, would do well to take the safer pitching wedge in this situation.

Grip

With either of the clubs just mentioned, you can reach the green easily. Therefore, you can shorten your grip by placing the hands well down on the shaft and still carry the distance required. The shortened grip increases your control and produces a steeper backswing. You want all the height you can get, so the club face must not be allowed to close. To guard against this, place both your hands slightly more to the left on the shaft than you would do for a normal pitch. Furthermore, the shortened grip makes you stand nearer the ball, ensuring a straighter and more upright swing that gets the ball high into the air.

The high, soft pitch

1. Take an open stance, with the ball placed inside the left heel and your weight favouring your *right* side. Your hands should be slightly turned to the left, low on the club and over the ball.

2. Without moving the body, turn the head and visualise the successful flight, bounce and roll of the ball. Good imagination leads to success.

Stance

Take your stance so that the ball is in line with the left heel. Keep your feet 10 – 12 in (25 – 30 cm) apart, with your weight slightly favouring the *right* side. The stance is open, with the left foot considerably withdrawn from the target line – about 6 in (15 cm). Keep the left hip pointing well to the left of the flag.

Posture

To facilitate a smooth swing movement through the ball, keep the knees bent so that you are almost in a sitting position. The hands should be directly above the ball (which should be in line with the left heel).

Movement

You will find that the movement back from the ball tends to be much straighter and may even be outside the target line. This depends on the stance and posture you have adopted and ensures that the club–ball contact is such that the ball flies high.

A full, free arm movement with an early wrist break will make sure the backswing is narrow and steep, enabling the club head to descend correctly to the ball, with the hands over the ball at impact, just as they were during address. This, together with the hand position and dominant left side, prevents the club face from closing prematurely. It also ensures that the club strikes the ball at the very bottom of the swing arc and continues through to the inside of the swing line with the left side leading, to give you all the height that is necessary.

3. Break your wrists early on the backswing to create a steep arc that will achieve increased height.

4. The shot has been played, with the left side leading to a high follow through that makes sure the movement is sufficient for the ball to reach the target.

The high, soft pitch is not such a difficult shot as many imagine. Of prime importance to its success are stance and set-up. The major difficulty is to remember that because the swing is so slow and produces little power, the length of the swing must be sufficient for the ball to reach the target. Therefore, you must practise the high, soft pitch often, until you have enough experience to know how long a swing you will need in each case.

Should you move the ball back in the stance, with your weight centred and the hands in the normal grip position, and use your arms more, your swing will be shallower, faster and more distinct. This will fly the ball further, in a lower trajectory, and with a considerable amount of back-spin.

So when playing downwind, use the softer, slower arm-and-wrist swing that will give a high trajectory with the ball falling softly on to the green. The wider, shorter and slightly faster backswing would give lower trajectory and more back-spin, which is preferable if you are playing into a strong headwind.

THE PITCHING GAME

An accurate approach shot can save at least one putt per hole, so it is well worth your while improving this part of your game. When you practise your pitching, be sure to write down the results in your notebook for reference when you are playing.

It is very important to get a clear mental picture of trajectory and flight for each type of pitch shot you play; therefore, practise only one type of pitch shot per session, so as not to confuse things.

Most changes that you can make to the flight and trajectory of the shot can be made at address, because the address position affects the shape, length and even the speed of the swing.

The waggle
As with all shots played in golf, the swing movement is instigated by a forward press. As the distance you want the ball to travel increases, a waggle or two prior to placing the club head behind the ball will help. The waggle (a preparatory mini-movement of the club head away from the ball) is made by flexing the left forearm and wrist to ensure that the backswing starts in the same manner. In other words, the waggle 'programs' you to start the backswing with the left arm moving the club head smoothly back, not by the right hand/arm pulling it away from the ball – this would alter the position of the club face as well as the swing line.

The waggle enhances overall smoothness of movement and is an important aid to starting the backswing at the correct tempo. (*Right*)

The waggles should keep the same tempo as the desired swing – sharp and direct when playing a short, distinct pitch over a bunker, but much slower and longer when preparing to play a soft, high pitch.

A final word of advice on pitching. Because the pitch shot is more intricate than the one-lever chip, never pitch when you can chip.

The pitching routine

Before playing the shot, imagine the trajectory, the landing point and the bounce and roll of the ball. Then take your practice swings in order to add 'feel'.

Make sure that the address position is correct for the type of pitch that you are about to play, and then swing the club, letting it do the work; on no account try to help the ball into the air – all that is needed are the correct stance and posture, together with a repeat of your practice swing.

When you play a high or normal pitch shot (slow or normal swing speed), the club should be swung freely, even at the slower speed, allowing the legs and hips to move in unison with the arms. The short-shafted address produces the more upright swing that is essential to good short-iron play around the green.

It is easier to judge the distance the ball will travel by the amount of swing movement rather than by club-head speed at impact. The best way to balance the length of the backswing with the length of the follow through is by the clock method. If you swing the arms on the backswing to nine o'clock, then your follow through should leave them in the three o'clock position. Similarly, a ten o'clock backswing should produce a two o'clock finish position.

Pitching drills

1 Practise this shot with your feet together. This will give you an idea of the length of flight you can expect from different lengths of swing, without using the body.

Any use of the upper body while you have the feet together will change the swing path radically, causing you to mis-hit the ball.

2 Starting with a swing speed that is less than your normal speed, let go of the club with your right hand as you finish the swing.

Repeat this several times, each time releasing the right hand earlier, until you are doing this just after the strike.

3 Repeat the sequence in step 2 above, only now your swing should have its normal speed. Release your right hand late in the follow through and then work back to release just after impact.

This drill is excellent for improving left-arm control of your swing, ensuring that the path of the swing is towards the target at impact. It may even help you to accomplish a slight draw, which is an important part of ball control and will prove very valuable later on in your golfing career.

CHAPTER SIX
THE PARTIAL SWING

As we have explained already, the average golfer should never play a full swing with the pitching wedge or sand iron, because such a movement is likely to lead to a loss of control, resulting in a shot that will not land and/or stop on the green.

Approach shots require accuracy and a half or three-quarter swing with less than full power will greatly improve the chances of pinpointing the flag. The average golfer's precision is less the more complete and full-powered the swing is; so, your chances of success will be greatly improved if you use a half or three-quarter swing with less than full power. Attempting a full swing with the pitching wedge when it is too difficult for your present standard will cause you only embarrassment and loss of strokes.

If a strong wind is blowing (especially if it is against you), or there is a considerable distance between the front edge of the green and the flag, or if your ball is lying badly, striking the ball high in the air all the way to the target and landing it near the flag becomes very difficult. A lower-flighted ball with a shorter and more controlled swing will always give you a better chance of success.

Therefore, choosing a partial swing increases your chances of striking the ball well and makes it easier to achieve the correct length and line. It is important that you practise the partial swing as often as possible in order to learn how altering your choice of club and/or swing length will achieve different distances. Practice and experience will help you build up a 'databank' of partial shots for every occasion, and you can save many strokes by calling on the correct shot for each particular situation that arises during a game.

The choice of club

As you have decided to use less movement than the full swing, the club must be 'strong' enough to reach the target despite the shorter swing. However, you must also consider the fact that the position of the ball in the stance and the reduced wrist movement will create a wider arc on the backswing, thus giving you a lower trajectory and a longer roll after landing.

Experience is the only teacher that is able to help you choose the right club, so when you practise this kind of shot, try out several clubs from the same lie, noting which club produces the correct trajectory and roll. Then when you meet this situation out on the course, your choice will be easier to make.

Grip

Hold the club firmly, 2 – 3 in (50 – 75 mm) from the top, with the pressure coming from the last three fingers of both hands. The firmness of your grip will reduce the amount of wrist movement (that is, you

Playing an approach shot with a half swing

This is a typical approach shot from a good lie on the fairway with a straight line to the green, and some 70 – 90 yds (65 – 80 m) to the flag. Accuracy is what you need here, and your big fear is that you will hit the ball too hard and send it bouncing over the green. But by carefully choosing the club – here, the No. 9 iron is the best bet – and by drawing on what practising the half swing with this club has taught you concerning height, bounce and roll, you can play this shot confidently up to the green and close to the flag. (Because you are using the No. 9 iron, the ball will not bounce and roll as much as it would if you chose a No. 6 or 7 iron. The steeper trajectory will make it stop more quickly.)

1. At address, stand with the ball back in the stance. Keep your hands firm on the shaft and in front of the ball.

2. A wide, controlled backswing, created mostly by the arms, approaches the ten o'clock position. Both feet are firmly on the ground.

won't hinge your wrists too much on the backswing), thus preventing the ball from flying too high.

Stance

Because you are using a longer club, the swing will be shorter, so the feet do not need to be so far apart as they would be for the full swing movement. Keep your weight more on the left foot than on the right. The ball is just right of centre and your hands should be in front of it.

Posture

Your posture depends very much on the distance you want to hit the ball, on prevailing wind conditions, and on your choice of club. The shorter grip causes you to stand nearer the ball with just a little knee flex. Keep your weight forwards on the balls of the feet (but more on the left foot than on the right) and the hips pointed slightly left of target (which tends to keep the movement firm and prevents the backswing being too long).

Movement

Swing the club low and wide on the backswing. The firmness of the grip will ensure that the wrists bend less than usual. The half backswing will take the arms to the nine o'clock position, while the three-quarter swing will take them to the ten o'clock position. On the downswing the club is returned to the ball with the left arm pulling close to the body in order to keep the club head on an inside path and behind the hands. The swing is very controlled and the finish position on the follow through (three o'clock or two o'clock) is a copy of the backswing.

The half and three-quarter swings are identical, apart from the length of the backswing and the follow through. You must decide yourself which of these partial shots to play, as the amount of movement required is dictated by how hard and from what direction the wind is blowing, by the distance you want the ball to fly, and by your choice of club.

3. Just after impact, the arms are swinging towards the target and the ball is on its way. The upper body is relatively still, while the club moves back to the inside of the target line.

4. A controlled finish, with the weight on the left foot and the right heel leaving the ground late in the follow through and the arms ending in the two o'clock position.

The three-quarter swing from a good lie

1. The ball has a good lie, some 90 yds (80 m) from the green and 30 yds (27 m) more to the flag, which is at the back of a long, upward-sloping green. A No. 6 or No. 7 iron is the right club for this particular shot.

2. Following the usual pre-swing routine, pick out the intermediate target and take your established number of practice swings to get the proper feel for the shot. (Compare this with photo 6 on the opposite page: the actual swing is an exact copy of the practice swing.)

3. Having completed your pre-swing routine, address the ball. Then using mainly your arms, take a wide three-quarter backswing, with the left heel on the ground and with your hands firm on the shaft to prevent too much wrist movement.

4. With left arm and side very much in control, swing the club back to the ball, arms leading and with the left arm close to the body to ensure a swing from the inside. *(Above)*

5. Arms flowing wide out to the target before moving inside and up to the three-quarter position. The finger pressure reduces wrist movement and keeps the ball low. *(Above right)*

6. When you have completed the follow through, your arms, hands and club should have the same position as they had on the backswing. Body weight well on the left foot and right knee turned inwards towards the target, causing your right heel to leave the ground. *(Right)*

A PARTIAL SWING FROM A DIVOT MARK

This shot is also known as the 'punch' shot.

If the ball is lying badly on the fairway (for instance, in a divot mark), you can play a punch shot to ensure that you strike the ball well. The punch shot is the same as the half or three-quarter swing just described, except that you stop the club early on in the follow through.

Be sure that your hands are in front of the ball at impact and that the arms, not the wrists, are used. The club should stop pointing at the target, with the toe of the club head pointing at the sky. Using the wrists in this shot, together with the early stop on the follow through, would result in the ball curving to the left in the air.

The punch shot, although not the easiest of shots to play, should be a part of your golfing arsenal. It can be used when playing from under trees, from bad lies and when playing from an elevated tee into a strong headwind. The correct choice of club, together with a strong but unhurried arm swing, will send the ball low and with plenty of roll.

It is vital that you use the arms only so as to prevent the club face closing before the ball is struck. As in all strong shots, if the club is stopped soon after impact, the ball may turn left in the air; so, be sure to practise the shot on the practice ground before playing it on the course.

Partial shots are not only the absolutely correct shot to play on certain occasions, but they also teach us that out on the golf course it is not always necessary to play a shot that makes you feel that you must exert yourself unduly.

Many weekend players would benefit if they played more three-quarter controlled shots instead of playing an exaggerated full swing movement at top speed.

Playing from a divot mark

1. The ball is lying in a divot mark on the fairway, making clean contact difficult. It is 120 yds (110 m) from the flag, which is again at the far end of a long green. A headwind causes further difficulty.

2. Choose your No. 6 iron. This will become a No. 5 iron when you have your hands in front of the ball and the ball is back in the stance. Take your practice swings as usual.

3. A half to three-quarter backswing with reduced wrist movement will allow you to get at the ball better when it is lying this badly.

4. A solid and unhurried movement through the ball, with the arms leading all the way, will send the ball low towards the target, bouncing before reaching the green and rolling up to the flag.

5. The right arm has added the necessary thrust and the hands are passive all the way. The arms are stretched and the shaft points towards the target, with the toe of the club pointing towards the sky and the left hip turned well out of the way.

CHAPTER SEVEN
THE FULL SWING

The full swing movement, properly carried out, will achieve optimum distance and direction with every club. It does not mean hitting the ball with full power. The swing movement is basically the same no matter which club you use, the only difference being that the swing plane is most upright for the No. 9 iron and least upright for the driver. The reasons are the length of shaft, the lie of the club, and the position of the ball in the stance. With the longer clubs, these factors will automatically cause you to stand further away from the ball, more upright, and with more upper body behind the ball. The further you stand from the ball, the flatter the swing will be, thus creating a shallower arc through the hitting area and sending the ball further.

Every club in your bag will give you a certain distance when the ball is struck correctly at a controlled speed with the same swing movement. Remember it is the target area that is important: a well played shot with a longer club will always give a better result than if you take a shorter club and force the swing in the vain hope of creating added length. Each change of club to a lower number will send the ball between 10 and 15 yds/m further, so try to swing every club at the same speed: avoid the trap of trying to hit the longer clubs harder.

For most people, 75% power with a complete swing movement will always give the best results. You never really need full power.

The full golf swing is the movement made when the club choice alone decides the height and length of the shot played. In other words, each individual golfer should have only one full swing movement; the different heights and lengths that he or she can achieve with this movement are dictated by the club used.

The important thing to remember about the full swing is that it is a fluid movement, not the moving of your club through a number of different positions. One thousand different positions will not create a successful golf swing, but the golf swing moves smoothly through a thousand positions!

Your pre-swing routine for all full swing shots is also the same, but your stance, posture and ball position will differ slightly, being dictated by your build, your personal swing and the length of club you have chosen for the shot.

Two very important factors should dominate the average golfer's use of the full swing: the first is that you must have a good mental picture of the shot to be played; the second is that you should always make a conservative choice of club. As you cannot expect to hit every shot 100%, you ought to choose a club that will reach the target when you swing comfortably within your capacity.

PRE-SWING ROUTINE

Do not take practice swings when you play the full swing movement. There are three reasons for this.

1 The full swing movement is too tiring.

2 After every full swing it takes time for the muscles to return to normal. It would delay the game unnecessarily and destroy your rhythm if you had to wait the required time after each practice swing.

3 The full swing movement is the same length every time, so there is little need to gauge the length of the backswing.

However, this does not mean that you must omit your pre-shot routine. It must be followed, with the following change.

After deciding that you need to play a full swing, pick out the intermediate target. Then make two or three 'mini-swings' (not more than one-quarter swings) at a slow pace, seeing all the while in your mind's eye the perfect flight, bounce and roll of the ball.

Now, before taking your stance, place the club head correctly behind the ball.

The full swing routine

1. First choose the target area. Which line will it take and how far can it be expected to fly? Once the line is picked out, the intermediate target is chosen.

A couple of preliminary waggles help you to sharpen up, then a forward press leads you smoothly into the backswing, in which the left hand and arm move the club head back and up. With the shorter irons, it is not necessary to have the shaft pointing straight at the target (parallel to the target line) at the top of the backswing, provided that the shoulders are free from tension. With the longer clubs, this tends to happen automatically.

2. Place the club carefully behind the ball, which is teed so that half of it is above the top of the club head, which in turn must be aligned directly with the intermediate target.

3. The stance is now taken and the feet and body are adjusted to the club and the ball.

4. The waggle brings the club head back along the swing path at the pace at which you are going to make the backswing. Remember, always make the same number of waggles.

5. The club is returned to the ball and the forward press is made, the right knee moving slightly in towards the left knee and the hands moving just past the ball.

6. The arms swing the club back from the ball in a low, wide arc at the same pace as the waggle.

7. A full, free swing with the arms causes the shoulders to turn and the weight to shift to the inside of the right foot. The left knee is pulled to the right, causing the left heel to lift.

8. As the left arm swings the club down on the inside, the weight shifts naturally back to the left foot.

9. Just after impact, the arms swing out after the ball, the left hip moving out of the way and the head slightly further back and lower than it was at address, due to the movement of the lower body.

10. The right side and shoulder are coming through and under, while the head has not yet moved.

11. The correct finish position: well balanced, the right foot perpendicular and the belt buckle pointing at the target.

THE FULL SWING MOVEMENT

The backswing

The full swing movement starts with a forward press that then moves smoothly into the backswing, straight back, low to the ground and wide. The club head moves first straight back from the ball and then inside the target line and up in a low and wide arc. This will cause the shoulders to turn, not 'tilt', on the correct plane. The plane of the shoulders during the backswing is always flatter than that described by the arms.

The width of the backswing is governed by the left arm because the right arm is bent at address. The absence of tension at address now causes the right arm to bend more; then the wrists start to hinge and as the arms continue up, the shoulders follow until the top of the backswing is reached. At this moment, the shaft should be parallel to the target line and nearly parallel to the ground.

Maintain the left hand well away from the body, thus keeping the radius of the swing constant. Retain enough pressure on the shaft with the left fingers to prevent it from losing contact with the heel of the left hand.

The arm movement has now turned the upper body so that the shoulders are 90° to the target line and the hips are turned only 45°; plus, most pressure is on the inside of your right foot and the right leg is in the same position as at address.

The turning of the body has also pulled the left leg so that the left knee points in towards the right and, for almost all players, causes the left heel to leave the ground. Trying to keep the left heel on the ground during a full swing is best left to professional tournament players.

If your stance and posture are correct, everything will move together in one piece and you will avoid unwanted independent action of the upper body while you maintain good contact between your feet and the ground. During the backswing, this contact restricts the movements of the thighs and legs, while the upper body is 'wound up'. (The winding up of the shoulders during the backswing is called 'torque' and is caused by the free arm movement against the lesser movement of the hips, which is in turn caused by the restricting movement of the legs.) This winding up creates *torsion*, not tension (absolutely not!).

Watch the professional players and you will see that they move their shoulders more and their hips less on the backswing than does the ordinary player, creating enormous pent-up energy. Of top professionals, only a very small handful stop at the top of the backswing; they show a noticeable bending of the left arm just then, proving that it is the centrifugal force of the swing that helps to keep the radius of the swing constant, not a conscious attempt at keeping the left arm straight. Smoothly and without rushing, the backswing moves into the downswing. If you keep the swing moving, the centrifugal force maintains the left arm fairly stretched, helping you to keep a constant radius.

So, the backswing creates and conserves energy by winding up the torso and putting the club in the correct plane and position, making it easier to swing the club with increasing speed back to the ball along the correct path and angle of descent. In other words, it is the energy that you create and conserve during your backswing that propels the ball on its way to the target.

In order to send the ball the required distance, you must have the correct position on the backswing so as to allow the full, free use of the golf club on the downswing, through the ball, to a finely balanced finish.

Many golfers ask if their left heel should lift slightly off the ground on the backswing (this is caused by the inward pointing of the left knee). The answer is that it is not mandatory but depends on your age, size and suppleness. Most people find it easier to allow the left heel to lift slightly, but you must ensure that you retain good contact between the inside of the left foot and the ground.

With the head behind the ball and the shoulders turned 90°, the swing centre is best imagined as your left shoulder. Should you feel that the swing centre is the breast bone, you are very likely to cause a reverse weight shift during the backswing, with most of your weight on the left foot instead of the right.

The path followed by the club head on the backswing is straight back from the ball, to the inside of the target line as the shoulders turn, then up as the arms continue to control the movement. The lower body follows last in the backswing sequence and acts as a stabilising force to conserve the power created by the winding up of the shoulders.

Although for 95% of all golfers there is no backswing position – the downswing starting from the lower body before the backswing is completed – the club should be parallel to the target line and in the correct plane before returning on the downswing. This allows the arms to play the major role, swinging the club down to and through the ball, unhindered by the body, causing power and length through the release and full use of the club.

The downswing

The changeover from the backswing to the downswing is probably the most discussed and least understood part of the full swing. For the majority of us there is no halt at the top of the backswing, so there can be no real start of the downswing – I think that it is best to regard the downswing as simply a change of direction.

All those who have been taught golf properly have learned that they should feel that they change direction during the swing by pulling the club *down* on the inside of the target line with both arms, the left arm leading and dominating. This will move the pressure over to the left foot automatically. Only now will the hips turn towards the target, bringing the weight of the left leg on to the left heel, leaving plenty of room for the arms to continue unhindered forwards, before returning the club head to the inside of the target line and up to the finish position.

Swinging down with the arms helps to prevent the body from getting in front of the ball, from which position it is impossible to strike the ball correctly. A free and purposeful arm swing down to the ball will allow the legs to move in unison with the arms, thus keeping the upper body behind the ball at impact.

The full swing movement

1. The address position with correct posture and stance. The position of the ball is well forwards in the stance. The weight favours the right side, which is lower than the left, and the upper body is behind the ball.

2. After the standard number of waggles and a forward press, the club head is swung low and wide back from the ball, with no independent wrist movement.

WARNING! Your natural reaction to a perfectly performed backswing is to start the downswing from the lower limbs. High-handicap players often swing the club head down to the ball too late, so any conscious effort to start the downswing with the legs will then leave the club head so far behind it will never catch up, resulting in a tremendous slice. Concentrate instead on swinging the arms down, so that you instinctively move the left hip out of the way, allowing the club to do its work.

If the backswing is performed 100% correctly, then a number of things occur quite naturally. The legs, having resisted the turn on the backswing, start towards the target automatically, causing a natural weight shift which returns the left heel to the ground and turns the hips to the left. Wonderful, you might think. But how many of us have a perfect backswing? With our backswings, most of us would do best to think only of swinging the club down to the ball with the arms and letting the weight transference occur 'by itself'. The transference of pressure from the right foot to the left heel should be a result of the left arm swinging first down and then from the inside to along the target line.

For most beginners, any conscious attempt to shift the weight first or to turn the hips to the left early will usually bring the club head to the ball very late and from the outside of the target line. This is the cause of many a sliced or topped shot, because the club head arrives at the ball after the upper body has turned to the left. Your partner will usually tell you that you looked up, but how can you stop your head from turning to the target if your shoulders are already turned towards it and the club head has still not reached the ball?

The strike position in a perfectly executed golf swing should differ only a little from the address position. The lower body will be slightly further forwards and more to the left; the head and right shoulder will be slightly lower and further back.

Your natural flexibility will allow you to swing the club head down with your arms, causing rising speed that maximises just before you hit the ball. If you swing the arms down first, before turning the shoulders, the release will occur quite naturally, with the pent-up energy coming from the full use of the club, sending the ball a long way with what you feel was a free and effortless swing.

Continued overleaf

3. Nearing the point where the change of direction occurs, the left knee points inwards, the left heel is raised, and the right leg position remains the same as it was at address. The body is well behind the ball and there is a full shoulder turn.

4. As the downswing neared the hitting area, the weight moved to the left foot and the arms swung down on an inside path at a shallow angle. The club head, approaching at a shallow angle, passes its lowest point before impact. The left hip has turned out of the way and the right heel is raised.

REMEMBER! The club must be swung down first and must approach the ball from the inside of the target line, while the upper body is held back in order to allow the club to do the work. In itself, this will help prevent that most common error of the club approaching the ball too steeply, too late and from the outside. Leaving the club head a long way behind is only worthwhile if you can make it catch up with the swing before the ball is struck, and that is something best left to the top golfers. If the club head comes too early to the ball, you may lose some of the effect; if it comes too late, you lose almost all of it.

The follow through

The finish position that you adopt after the ball has been struck cannot in itself affect the flight of the ball, but what you do after the ball has been struck is always the result of what occurred earlier. A free, flowing swing devoid of tension will allow the club to continue after the strike. The idea is to swing the club to the target and not at the ball. Swing *through* the ball, not at it. The amount of swing movement after ball contact depends on arm freedom and club-head speed. Remember to swing the club, not yourself, to the finish position.

The movement of the arms around the axis of the swing will turn the body to the finish position, facing the target with the right knee pulled forwards towards the left leg and your belt buckle pointing at the target. The pressure has now transferred to the left heel.

Do not mistake weight transference with moving your upper body. Your weight can be on the left foot and your body still behind the shot.

At the end of the full swing movement, it is the free swinging of the arms in the correct plane and along the correct path that produces a good follow through, with perfect control and balance. The pressure should be on the left foot, belt buckle turned towards the target, and head and shoulders behind the lower body, causing a bowing forwards of the left leg and a slight backward bowing of the spine; only the toes of the right foot touch the ground and the right foot is perpendicular.

Juniors often exaggerate this finish position, using a violent leg movement from a wide stance. Older golfers find this position difficult, so a narrower stance and a freer use of the arms, hands and club will help them maintain control and balance during a full follow through.

The full swing movement, cont. _____

5. The ball is on its way, the arms extend after the ball and the lower body position causes the arms to swing from along to inside the target line. The head is still well back.

6. The finish position. The arms have pulled the body round so that it faces the target, and although the weight has moved on to the left heel, the shoulders are still behind the shot, creating balance and control.

Change of swing plane

In a correctly executed golf swing, there is a noticeable change of swing plane between the backswing and the downswing. (Swing plane, as we have said, is the angle of the swing arc to the ground.) The club is swung back from the ball and then inside the target line and up. However, it does not return to the ball on the same plane, but rather on a flatter plane, caused by the leg and hip movement to the left at the same time as the arms pull the club down on the inside.

1. The backswing position with a middle iron. The weight is on the right foot, the shaft is parallel with the target line and in the correct plane. The club face is correctly positioned.

2. The downswing is under way, with the weight moving on to the left foot and the lower body turning as the club is pulled down on the inside of the target line, creating a flatter plane.

3. After the strike, the weight is on the left foot, the hips have moved through the shot, the right knee into the left, and the arms swing inside and across the chest, while the upper body is still well back.

4. The follow through is completed. The arms are well round to the inside, pulling the body into a position where the weight is on the left heel, with the right foot perpendicular and the shoulders fully square to the target.

Swing plane

Illustrated here are the address positions and the consequent backswings for four different clubs. You can see from these photos that the nearer you stand to the ball, the more you bend forwards and the more upright is the backswing. Furthermore, the shorter irons cause a more downward blow, while the longer clubs (which have the ball forwards in the stance) have a shallower downward angle and a more forward movement into the hitting area.

1. Address position with the No. 9 iron: close to the ball.

2. Backswing with the No. 9 iron. The swing is quite upright.

3. Address position with the No. 6 iron: less close to the ball.

4. Backswing with the No. 6 iron. The swing is less upright.

5. Address position with the No. 4 iron: further from the ball.

6. Backswing with the No. 4 iron. Swing is flatter.

7. Address position with the No. 3 wood: furthest from the ball.

8. Backswing with the No. 3 wood. Swing is flattest.

THE FULL SWING WITH THE SHORT IRONS

The short irons (the Nos 7, 8 and 9 irons) are used when accuracy is at a premium. The ball should be struck just before the bottom of the swing arc, with a steeply descending club head. The line that the club head follows in the forward swing is down from the inside to along (where contact takes place) to inside, and up at the finish.

Due to the fact that the short irons are shorter-shafted and more lofted, play them with a different stance and posture than you adopt when playing the longer clubs. Standing nearer the ball creates a more upright plane, with less body movement and with the feeling that it is mostly the arms and hands that are employed during the swing. This type of swing produces an air of great authority and crispness. The ball is struck first, and then the ground, taking turf.

The full swing movement with the short irons is still primarily a precision shot because the amount of back-spin helps to keep the ball on line. The pitching wedge should never be used for a full swing (greater accuracy can be achieved more easily with the No. 9 iron and a three-quarter swing). The short irons are fairly easy to use and are therefore popular with all golfers.

Grip

The grip used for the full swing with the short irons is the normal one, but the club is never held at the extreme end of the shaft. Depending on the lie and the height required, the clubs are held lower down on the shaft.

Stance

Since the arm movement is now a full swing, which turns the shoulders, bringing your weight more on to the inside edge of the right foot during the backswing, the feet must be far enough apart and slightly open to allow for all this extra movement

The full swing with the short irons

When playing the short irons, it is not enough just to aim at the green: here you are going for the flag. Precision is the key word.

1. The stance is marginally open and rather narrow, with just a fraction more weight on the right foot. Because you are standing near the ball, the swing will be upright.

2. The backswing is very controlled – primarily an arm and hand movement – but wide and long enough to bring the weight on to the inside of the right foot.

and to give you balance. But you must not have too wide a stance, as this would inhibit the free swinging of the arms. I myself have about 20 in (50 cm) between my feet when playing this kind of shot, but every player must work out the optimum distance that is suitable for his or her own size, swing, etc.

Note that on the backswing the weight is transferred to the inside edge of the right foot, never to the outside edge!

Posture

When you address the ball, bend forwards from the waist with your weight on the soles of the feet and the arms hanging freely from the shoulders. The ball position is in the centre of the stance. The right side of your body (shoulder and elbow) is lower than your left, putting about 60% of your body mass and weight to the right of the ball. The club shaft points at the left groin and the hands are in front of the ball. There is a distinct angle between the hanging arms and the plane of the shaft.

Your stance and posture (if correct, that is, as described above) will produce an upright swing plane; this encourages a steep return of the club head to the ball, giving the ball a high trajectory.

Provided that the shoulders are free of tension, the upright swing plane will turn them enough to allow the lower body to trigger off the downswing automatically. This allows you to swing the club head freely through the ball to a perfectly balanced finish, with the hands high and the club allowed to continue until the shaft points upwards. In the finish position, the waist is turned fully towards the target, but the head and shoulders are still behind where the ball was at address, and you look at the ball flight from 'underneath'. In the finish position, your body weight has transferred to the left heel and right toe.

Take turf with the short irons when you use the full swing movement. Because the swing plane is upright and the ball is in the centre of the stance, it will be struck a descending blow and turf should be taken after impact.

3. The arms have been swung steeply down on the inside of the target line, turf has been taken, and now the arms flow freely to the inside with the upper body just behind the strike position.

4. The arms have continued up and around, pulling the body to a perfectly balanced finish position, facing the target and with the right foot perpendicular.

THE FULL SWING WITH THE MEDIUM IRONS

The Nos 4, 5 and 6 irons are those most likely to be used by the average player for transport shots and for the shorter shots from the tee. With the exception of the No. 4 iron, most players enjoy using them. Balls struck with these clubs seem to have the best chance of flying fairly straight and a considerable distance. The amount of back-spin created usually produces a straight ball flight, and even if this does not occur, the middle irons can somehow get the ball in the vicinity of the green.

The change in ball position, stance and posture, due to the fact that the medium irons are longer, now creates a slightly less upright swing plane; as a result the club is not returned to the ball so steeply. The club is still descending when the ball is struck but less so than with the shorter irons. The loft of the club convinces us that all that is necessary for a good shot is to swing the club so that the lowest part of the swing arc comes just after impact. This time, only a little turf is taken.

THE FULL SWING WITH THE LONG IRONS

It is with the long irons that anxiety and fear raise their ugly heads. The Nos 1, 2 and 3 irons don't seem strong enough to send the ball any distance at all, while the loft in no way looks sufficient to get the ball airborne. These clubs simply don't convince the high-handicap golfer that a normal swing is sufficient.

Placing the ball further forwards in the stance and further away from you will produce a flatter swing, whereby the club head will approach the ball in a much shallower arc. The ball is almost brushed off the grass. You will be surprised to see that, despite your doubts, the club is well equipped to send the ball flying a long way if you use your normal swing speed and achieve good ball contact.

Whether the ball is teed or on the ground, shots with the long irons are always played in the same manner.

The long irons often present a problem for the average golfer. A long iron gives a fragile impression; you feel it necessary both to hit the ball hard and to help it up into the air. But if you swing your long club with the same tempo as, say, your No. 7 iron, you are sure to achieve more satisfactory results, the ball flying high enough and further than you imagined.

The object of the swing with one of the long irons is to send the ball further while retaining as much accuracy as possible. A proper swing with the right tempo is important. Don't grasp the club tightly, tense your arm and shoulder muscles, nor after a short, quick backswing, 'throw yourself' at the ball. Approach the ball calmly and examine the lie. Ask yourself which club will enable you to reach the green with a normal swing. Can you land the ball short of the green and have it bounce forwards on to the putting surface? Or is the landing area so difficult to hit that it would be better to take a middle iron and leave yourself a simple pitch or chip on to the green, ensuring that you do not lose another stroke?

Once you decide that the long iron is what you are going to play, do not take any full practice swings. As we have already pointed out, this is too tiring. Instead, swing the club back and forth at about hip height and at half speed, feeling the looseness of your arms, before placing the club head behind the ball, aimed at the intermediate target.

Grip
Hold the club in the normal manner, slightly down on the shaft and without increasing grip pressure. The top of the shaft should protrude above the base of the left hand. Never hold the club at the very top of the shaft.

Stance
The longer the distance you want to send the ball, the further your feet should be

apart. (Because the longer club moves through a bigger and wider arc, more body movement is caused, and this requires a more stable base.) The actual distance between your feet is a personal matter and depends on your size, weight, shape and age. It must be wide enough to give you a solid base for the bigger movement, but not so wide as to restrict the free turning of the body. I would suggest about 14 in (35 cm). A beginner might prefer less distance between his or her feet, as this encourages a freer movement and a bigger shoulder turn on the backswing.

Posture

Even though your weight is on the balls of the feet and the upper body is bent slightly forwards from the waist, the longer club means that you stand further away from the ball and also that the upper body is more upright than when you are playing the middle or shorter irons. The distance to the ball also causes a flatter swing plane.

With the club head placed behind the ball and pointing directly at the inter-mediate target, hold the club shaft so that it is pointing at the left groin. This makes you stand with the ball forwards (left of centre) in the stance, with the head behind the ball and with more weight on the right foot. It is essential that the upper body is still parallel to the target line, despite the fact that the ball is to the left of centre. This can only be achieved by ensuring that the right shoulder is lower than the left.

Allow the arms to hang naturally from the shoulders, with the right elbow soft and nearer the body than the left. The knees are flexed slightly, as with all full swing movements, and the right knee is inclined slightly towards the left leg.

THE FULL SWING WITH THE WOODEN CLUBS

The wooden clubs are either loved or hated, but there is no denying that few shots are so satisfactory and give so marked a sense of pleasure as the well-struck wood

shot. Watching the ball disappearing straight to the target, you may be tempted to wonder why you didn't hit it a little harder; then when you try, the result is always a disaster. The wooden clubs, like all others, are made to be swung freely, not hard. A full, free swing that results in a good shot feels exactly as it should – effortless.

When you are using the long clubs, the ball is further forwards in the stance. This will help you to sweep the ball off the grass with a feeling of complete smoothness. The ball is struck just before or at the bottom of the swing arc, which sends it away towards the target on a rising trajectory. The swing is full and unhurried, with complete freedom of arm movement.

THE WOODEN CLUBS FROM THE FAIRWAY

The shot from the fairway with a wooden club is a transport shot that should send the ball into a given target area from where you will have a straightforward pitch or chip on to the green. The average golfer should not attempt to pinpoint the green with this club but should concentrate on a particular target area.

Stance and posture for the wooden clubs from a fairway lie differ only a little from the stance and posture adopted for the long irons. The stance is a little wider and the body position is even more behind the ball, thus giving an even shallower arc on the forward swing, sweeping the ball from the grass on a lower trajectory and making it go further.

It might be advisable to practise fairway wood shots before practising fairway shots with the long irons, because the size of the wooden club head makes it appear more suitable for sending the ball a long way. With long irons, you may feel the need to try to hit the ball harder. Practice with the wooden club will help you to create a smoother swing, which you can use then with the long irons.

Grip

Hold the club normally with the little finger of the left hand about ¹/₂ in (12 mm) from the top of the shaft. Never hold the club at the very end of the shaft. The grip pressure should come predominantly from the last three fingers of the left hand and the middle two fingers of the right.

Stance

As for all shots, keep your weight on the balls of the feet, which should be about the width of the shoulders apart; as for all longer clubs, your weight should favour the right side. The ball is forwards in the stance.

Posture

Due to the fact that the wooden club is so long, you stand with a more upright posture. The swing plane is flatter because you stand further away from the ball.

Check very carefully that the club shaft is pointing at the left groin and that the club face is square to the intermediate target, thus helping you to place the feet correctly in relation to the ball (in this case, the ball is further forwards in the stance). Let the arms hang freely from the shoulders, which must be parallel to the target line.

The more the ball is forwards in the stance, the more you must think of keeping the shoulders parallel to the target line. When the ball is forwards in the stance, it is easy to commit the cardinal sin of addressing the ball with the shoulders turned to the left of the target line, instead of dropping the right shoulder to ensure that the important parallel line is maintained.

Swing movement

Start with a forward press that continues into a full swing movement in which, at the top of the backswing, the shaft should be pointing parallel both to the target line and the ground, before returning down on the inside of the target line to the ball. With the ball placed forwards in the stance, the club head will now approach along a shallower arc, reaching its lowest point on or just after contact, giving the impression that the ball is swept away with a continuous, smooth movement.

Allow the hands and club to continue all the way with the club still in the same plane and the hips nearer the target than any other part of the torso. The head and back should be slightly arched away from the target, the head looking up at the flight of the ball from underneath. This position

The full swing with the wooden clubs

Fairway wood
Using the longer clubs, which will automatically send the ball further, means that you have to make some slight changes to the stance and posture. The very fact that the club is longer causes you to stand further away, more to the right and with more weight on the right foot, meaning that you are going to strike the ball with a shallower arc. Equally so, the wider and longer swing requires more body movement than the shorter clubs do. Therefore, the stance must be wider. Also, the length of the club causes the posture to be more upright, which creates a flatter shoulder turn than you get with the shorter clubs.

1. The stance for the fairway wood is wide enough to create a solid base for the increase in body movement demanded by this swing. The ball is well forwards in the stance and more weight is on the right foot. You must be certain that your shoulders are parallel to the target line.

can be practised easiest from an uphill lie, which assists in keeping the upper body behind the ball, even when you have reached the follow-through position.

As with all full swing movements, the club should swing freely and smoothly from start to finish, with the momentum of the club head increasing gradually as it approaches the ball. Remember to use the same tempo as for the short clubs.

2. The backswing. The arms have swung the club low and wide from the ball, causing first the shoulders and then the lower body to turn. Your weight moves to the inside of your right foot and the right leg position stays the same as at address. The full turning of the shoulders has caused the left knee to bend more to the right than it does with the shorter club swing, bringing the left heel well off the ground.

3. The ball has been swept away and, because of the greater distance to the ball at address, the arms now swing *well* to the left after impact, keeping the swing plane constant. There is lots of lower body movement here, but the head is still well back.

4. The follow through. The momentum of the swing has now pulled both the body and the head to a full and perfectly balanced finish position, with chest and hips facing the target.

TEE SHOTS WITH THE WOODEN CLUB

All full golf swings, including the tee shots, must be played with a target area in mind. The target area must be so large that a shot that is less than perfect will still put the ball somewhere within it. When the first shot lands anywhere in the target area, you can play the second shot with a normal swing too, without looking for your ball in the woods or rough. Have a realistic and conservative landing area in mind when you plan the tee shot, so that the second shot can be played from a good lie on the fairway.

Tee up the ball so that half of it is above the top edge of the club head. The stance and set-up are the same as for the wooden shots from the fairway, except that the ball is a little further forwards in the stance and the feet are a little wider apart. This, together with more weight on the right foot, allows you to strike the ball after the club head has reached its lowest point on the downswing. In fact, the ball is struck very slightly on the upswing.

The great danger when playing wooden shots from the tee is that you tighten the arm and shoulder muscles, thinking that this will send the ball further... it won't ! All it will do is shorten the backswing, causing loss of rhythm and a faulty upper body movement that then causes the shoulders to turn to the target too early, resulting in a slice or, even worse, a topped shot.

Be sure with all full swing movements to use your imagination, see a successful result, go through your normal pre-swing routine, and above all swing the club freely and smoothly from the address position to a well balanced finish of the follow through. Your overriding thought should be of a fluid movement, not of the number of positions through which you are swinging the club.

The tee shot routine

1. One or two mini-swings back and forth just to loosen up and relax the muscles.

2. Stand behind the ball and choose a suitable intermediate target, a club length in front of the ball.

3. First place the club head behind the ball, pointing it at the intermediate target before taking up your stance.

4. With the stance taken, check that the club is still in the correct position and that your eyeline, shoulders, hips, knees and feet are parallel to the target line.

5. Preparatory to starting the backswing, make your usual number of waggles, at the speed at which you intend to start the backswing.

6. The ball is struck and on its way. Hips have moved out of the way to the left to allow the arms to continue from the target line to the inside before moving up.

7. The swing is completed by a well balanced and fully relaxed follow through.

CHAPTER EIGHT
THE SAND GAME

The sand shot is often considered the toughest of them all. No matter how well you play golf, you cannot avoid getting into sand now and then. It may be due to an unlucky bounce or you may simply have played a bad shot – it makes no difference, you still have to play the ball out of that bunker!

The object of shots from the sand is always the same: to see to it that the next shot is as simple as possible and to try to avoid losing a stroke.

It is essential that you practise sand shots as often as you can. Practice will give you experience; from experience you will gain knowledge. To play sand shots successfully, you must know how the club functions as it works its way through the sand and how the ball will fly when you 'splash' both sand and ball into the air. This knowledge will help you to approach any normal bunker shot with confidence.

The sand iron is different from the other irons. If you use an ordinary iron to play a shot from soft sand, it will dig in and stop abruptly, leaving the ball in the sand. The sand iron is built to bounce through the sand, displacing and compressing it behind the ball so that the sand and ball are 'splashed' into the air. Don't hit the ball, hit the sand. Furthermore, the sand cushions the power of the swing, so that the ball comes out softly.

When the shaft is upright, the trailing edge (also known as the 'flange' or 'bounce') of the sole is lower than the leading edge, enabling the club to bounce through the sand. This distinguishes the sand iron from all the other clubs. With its average loft of 56°, it is the most lofted of all clubs, enabling you to play quickly-rising, high shots.

The sand iron

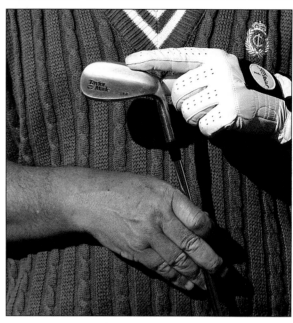

1. The sole of the sand iron is much wider than that of the other clubs and is noticeably convex. (Remember that the sand iron can be used to advantage in other situations too, e.g. in the rough.)

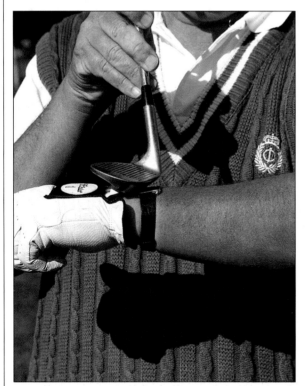

2. This photograph shows how the trailing edge of the sole is closer to the ground than is the leading edge. The more the club is opened, the lower the trailing edge will be and the easier it will bounce through the sand.

3. When the club is open the shaft is nearer the ball and there is a danger of hitting it with the hosel. To avoid this, address the ball off the toe of the club, as shown.

A GOOD LIE IN A GREENSIDE BUNKER WITH NORMAL SAND

Learn how to play this shot so that the ball finishes close to the flag and you will save many strokes.

Grip

Except for one very important difference, hold the club with the normal grip about 2 – 3 in (50 – 75 mm) down the shaft. The essential difference is that the club face is not square to the target, but open (i.e., turned to the right), and this is done before you place the hands on the club. Do this before you get into the sand bunker because you need to ground the club in the open position before you can place the hands on the shaft properly.

Opening the club face lowers the trailing edge even more, causing the club to bounce through the sand instead of digging in. The ball will be propelled then by the displacement of the sand behind it, softly, slowly, and with a considerable amount of height, ensuring that the ball stops shortly after landing.

Stance

Plant the feet securely in the sand with your whole body aligned to the left of the target – that is, with an open stance. This stance, when combined with the open club face, will create the height that the ball flies. The more the feet are aligned to the

From a good lie in a greenside bunker with normal sand

1. When you open the blade to create more bounce and height, you must do it outside the bunker and before you actually grip the shaft. Otherwise, there is a danger that the blade will return to square before impact.

2. Take your practice swings outside the bunker too, because you may not ground the club in the sand (two-stroke penalty!). The practice swings give you the right feel for the swing and allow you to visualise the successful result.

left and the more the club face is open (aligned to the right), the higher and shorter the ball will travel.

When you have learned to face your whole body the same angle to the left as the club face is pointing to the right, control of distance becomes easier.

Keep your weight centred, with the ball in line with the left heel and addressed towards the toe of the sand iron. When playing, do not ground the club in the bunker. When first practising this shot, lay your club head softly on the sand, as this will increase your confidence. (If you hold the club in the air from the beginning, it is difficult to know where to strike the sand.)

Posture

Keep the knees flexed and the body relaxed. The hands should be hanging freely from the shoulders, very slightly in front of the ball, and the club should not, of course, touch the sand.

Swing movement

The grip, stance and posture promote a swing that will take a long, shallow 'divot' of sand and compress it behind the ball, propelling it out of the bunker. The swing itself is very upright, rather long, and very much slower than you would expect necessary. Watch professionals playing this shot and you will think that they are trying to

From a good lie in a greenside bunker with normal sand, cont. _____

3. Ball in line with the left instep; feet, hips and shoulders point to left of target as much as club is open to right; weight centred. The ball is towards the toe of the club.

4. With a light grip and an early wrist break, take a full, free backswing. The tempo should be easy throughout. Leg action on the backswing is minimal. Left arm/hand dominates as usual.

play in slow motion. The line of the swing follows the stance – that is, to the left of the target. The arms lead the downswing all the way. The ball will come out of the bunker about halfway between where you have swung the club and where the blade was pointing when the club hit the sand.

Until you are proficient at this, it is a good idea to follow through to a high finish by concentrating on continuing the movement of the left side, with a distinct feeling of pulling the left arm to the left. This will stop the right hand from taking over and closing the club face, which should be pointing to the sky until near the end of the swing.

Even when playing very short shots, with the flag close to the edge of the bunker, it is better in the beginning to play the high follow through with a slower swing to be certain of getting out of the bunker and on to the green. Eventually, when you have gained enough confidence, you can stop the club earlier and lower to the ground, reducing the distance the ball travels.

5. Just after impact. The compressed sand is 'splashed' out of the bunker, lifting the ball high and softly over the front lip of the bunker.

6. The full follow through should leave you in a well balanced position. Swing exactly as if it were a normal golf shot. The result: perfect! All that is left is a simple putt.

FROM HARD SAND IN A GREENSIDE BUNKER

This type of sand shot differs from the others insofar as you should hit the ball first and not the sand.

If rain has packed the sand in a bunker, the sand iron will bounce on the surface rather than go into the sand. This means that the ball will be struck halfway up, making it hit the wall of the bunker or fly low and hard over the green. The trailing edge will not move any sand at all if the sand is hard, so you must avoid striking the sand before making contact with the ball. Therefore, don't choose a sand iron but take the pitching wedge instead and use a similar shot to the short pitch over a bunker. (Go back to Chapter Five and compare – there are many similarities.) The idea is the same, too – to 'pinch' the ball at the very bottom of the swing.

Grip
Hold the pitching wedge 2 in (5 cm) down on the shaft, with firm pressure from both hands but slightly more coming from the left fingers. Check that the blade is square with the intermediate target and close to the base of the ball (but not touching it or the sand).

Stance
Stand with about 8 – 10 in (20 – 25 cm) between the feet so that the ball is centred in the stance. The feet should be slightly open (pointing a little towards the intermediate target).

Posture
Flex the knees very slightly and hold the club with the hands directly over the ball.

Swing movement
Take a short backswing, about chest high, with very early wrist break to create a steep and high backswing arc. The downswing is initiated by pulling the club down with the left arm, the right arm passing in a flipping action directly under the stretched left arm shortly after impact. Allow the right knee to follow the swing to ensure that there will be increased weight on the left foot. Because the body is virtually still and the follow through is curtailed, the ball is pinched, giving it plenty of back-spin to stop it quickly after landing.

This shot, although appearing to be slow and lazy, creates a great deal of its effect by the fact that the ball is struck by the club and not by the sand. The hit-and-stop action, with the right hand flipping under the stretched left arm, imparts back-spin, so even if the ball comes out strongly, it will stop very soon after landing.

Short pitch from packed sand

Make practice swings outside the bunker, as you are not allowed to touch the ground in a bunker.

1. Hold the pitching wedge firmly, with a shortened grip. The club blade is near the base of the ball. Your weight is centred, stance slightly open and hands directly above the ball.

2. Break the wrists early to make a short, steep backswing. Your weight is still centred and your foot and knee positions are unaltered.

3. Pull the club down with the left arm, and at contact the ball is pinched due to the right hand passing under the stretched left arm.

4. The right knee is allowed to follow forwards, even though the club is stopped shortly after impact. This produces maximum spin.

PLAYING FROM A HALF-BURIED LIE IN A GREENSIDE BUNKER

Should the ball be half-buried in the sand, you may very easily get too much sand between the club head and the ball, or your club head may bounce and strike the top of the ball. Both these shots would leave the ball in the sand. To avoid this, you need to make some adjustments.

When the ball is lying half-buried, two things are necessary. At impact, there must be less sand than usual between the club face and the ball, and the club head must penetrate deeper into the sand. In other words, the club should not bounce through the sand but should dig into it.

Grip

Although you use the normal grip, you now want the club face to be square or closed (depending on the texture of the sand and how deep the ball is in it). Hold the club more firmly than usual about 2 in (5 cm) down the shaft.

Stance

The stance is square, with the feet firmly anchored in the sand to prevent slipping. With the blade square and the ball well inside the left heel, keep your weight predominantly on the left foot.

Posture

The shot is much more aggressive than the normal sand shot; therefore the knees and arms are less relaxed (don't allow any slackness to creep in). The hands and upper body are well in front of the ball, which results in a very steep entry into the sand.

Swing movement

Swing the club back from the ball steeply by cocking the wrists as early as possible on the backswing. On the downswing, swing the club with the hands and wrists so that the club enters the sand just behind the ball, popping it out.

This swing is short, sharp and direct, with body weight on the left foot throughout the whole movement. The deep penetration of the sand curtails the

The half-buried lie

1. After practice swings outside the bunker (with square blade), address the half-buried ball with it well inside your left heel, and your club face and feet square to the intermediate target. Your weight favours the left foot. Hands are in front of the ball.

follow through and the club often stops in the sand.

A lie such as this can be frightening for the faint-hearted, but don't let it put you off – simply remember the following. The downswing is very steep so there won't be much sand between club head and ball to soften the effect. This means that the ball will come out lower and faster than for a good lie (*see* above). Therefore, when you strike the sand near the ball don't apply so much force, otherwise it will come out too far and will roll a considerable distance as well.

2. An earlier wrist break and a firmer grip than for the good-lie shot. Use plenty of wrist when swinging the club head steeply down into the sand just behind the ball.

3. At impact, the sand propels the ball softly over the intermediate target and on to the green, where it rolls towards the flag. The square blade and firmer grip have 'splashed' the sand and ball up into the air.

Remember that this shot produces more roll because of the increased amount of sand between club face and ball.

THE BURIED LIE

Should the ball be almost completely buried, as it can easily be if the sand is soft and the ball comes in from a high trajectory, make a few slight adjustments to the way you handled the half-buried lie.

Grip
First, close the club before taking your grip, with the toe of the club nearly pointing at the ball and with the hands directly over it. Hold the club quite firmly and a good 3 in (75 mm) down the shaft.

Stance
The ball should be back of centre in the stance, which should be closed – that is, the right foot is drawn back about 8 – 10 in (20 – 25 cm). Your weight should be well on the left foot.

Posture
Keep the knees and arms less relaxed than normal, with the upper body and hands well in front of the ball.

Swing movement
Start the swing by cocking the wrists immediately at the beginning of a short, abrupt backswing. Hit down into the sand at the very back of the ball. The club will have displaced sufficient sand to send the ball out of the bunker, often leaving the club head still in the sand.

Once again, the ball will come out low and without back-spin, so if there is a high bank in front of the buried ball, play out of the bunker where the lip is low enough to ensure that the ball does not remain in the bunker.

The buried lie in a greenside bunker

1. The ball has landed in the bunker from a high trajectory and is plugged in soft sand.

2. Take the stance outside the bunker with the club face closed. Then place your hands about 3 in (75 mm) down the club shaft. Your toe line should point as much to the right as the club face is pointing to the left. Make practice swings as usual.

3. Now, retaining this grip, go into the bunker and adopt the same stance. Work the feet deep into the sand to give balance. The soles of the shoes should be below the level of the ball. (*Above*)

4. A short and very upright backswing with lots of wrist cock and a stable foot position starts off the swing movement. (*Above right*)

5. Swing the closed club head on a steep path into the sand just behind the ball. Hit down and let the wrists and club do the work. Be prepared for considerable roll, as the ball will have very little back-spin.

PUTTING FROM THE SAND

If the ball is lying on packed sand and there is no lip to the bunker, you may be able to putt the ball out with considerable accuracy. Everything is exactly the same as when you putt from off the green (Chapter Two), with sufficient movement to be sure to come out of the bunker. Don't try to hit the ball harder; if you do, you will end up striking it badly. Remember, it is the length of the backswing that should dictate the length the ball will travel.

Putting from the sand is not difficult if you remember the following. Take your practice swings outside the bunker in order to judge the length of swing required to ensure that the ball rolls out of the bunker.

Use the normal putting grip. Keep the hands and weight well forwards to the left, with the body absolutely still. The practice swings will have told you how long a backswing you need.

Follow your usual putting routine, but don't ground the club, and be sure to make the swing with your body still and your eye on the back of the ball.

Putting from the sand

1. Take your practice swings outside the bunker, gauging the length of backswing needed. It will be rather longer than you imagined – you do not want to increase the speed of the swing or move on the forward swing. (*Below left*)

2. Take up your stance with the weight mainly on the left foot and the hands in front of the ball. Address the ball one-third of the way up to avoid touching the sand. (*Below right*)

3. Be sure to repeat the long backswing of your practice swing. Do not hurry the downswing but maintain a smooth rhythm, keeping the body still and the eyes on the back of the ball.

4. Strike the ball with a smooth forward movement, keeping the head still and the eyes on where the ball was until well after the strike.

5. The ball has rolled up the bank of hard sand and continued to finish near the flag. A wise decision has saved you a stroke.

SHOTS FROM FAIRWAY BUNKERS

As your golf improves and you start sending the ball further from the tee, you might find yourself in a fairway bunker, still some considerable distance from the green. Should the lip of the bunker be fairly low (they usually are on fairway bunkers), your choice of club will depend on the lie of the ball and the distance required.

But a word of warning. No matter what club you use, it must have sufficient loft (even when you de-loft it by having your hands in front of the ball) to clear the front lip of the bunker. If the ball is still in the bunker after the shot, nine times out of ten it is because you have chosen a club that was not lofted enough. So choose your club with care. It is better to take a No. 7 iron and be 20 yds/m short of the green than to take a No. 5 iron and not get out of the bunker at all!

PLAYING AN IRON FROM A FAIRWAY BUNKER

If you have a bad lie in a fairway bunker, it is better to take the sand iron and 'splash' the ball safely back on to the fairway, rather than to take one of the other irons and go for length. However, if you have a decent lie choose a safe, lofted iron, say the No. 7.

Grip
Hold the club with the normal grip 1/2 in (12 mm) from the top. Take your practice swings outside the bunker to create feel for the precision in strike necessary to hit the ball cleanly.

Iron shots from a fairway bunker _____

1. A No. 7 iron is a good choice for this kind of shot. Take the stance with hands in front of the ball, which is well back in the stance. The club face should be slightly open. The right foot is angled into the sand and the right knee is flexed inwards to assist stability.

2. The backswing is completed. The arms swing freely, while the weight is centred and the right knee position constant.

Stance

Take your stance as for a normal shot with a middle iron, with both feet planted securely in the sand, but with the right angled markedly inwards, so as to provide a solid base for the backswing. This is to stop you moving during the backswing.

Hold the club in the air, just behind the ball, with the aim slightly to the left because the weight on the left foot will cause the ball to turn right in the air. The ball is just back of centre to facilitate striking the ball without contacting the sand.

Posture

Keep the hands and arms in front of the ball and place your weight primarily on the left foot. Maintain the knees very slightly flexed, giving you the feeling that you are standing high.

Swing movement

The normal backswing will tend to be more upright than usual, because the hands are in front of the ball and your weight is more on the left foot. Therefore, the club head will not touch the sand as you bring it back from the address position.

The reduced knee flex and angled right foot position will assist you to stand stably during the backswing. The downswing should be unhurried, concentrating on striking the ball and taking as little sand as possible before continuing to a full, controlled and well-balanced follow through.

3. The ball is struck first and very little sand is taken, so that the arms continue up and to the inside, with the upper body still behind where the ball was positioned.

4. The follow through is completed. The weight is now on the left foot, the hips are turned to the target and balance and poise have been maintained through good rhythm.

WOOD SHOT FROM A FAIRWAY BUNKER

Should the ball be sitting very well and the sand be not too soft, it may be possible to use a lofted wooden club (the 4, 5 or 7 wood) from the bunker.

Grip
Make sure that the club head is open before taking your grip. Remember to take your practice swings outside the bunker to create feel for the shot you are about to play.

Stance
Plant the feet firmly in the sand, with the right foot angled inwards to assist stability. The ball is played slightly less forwards than usual, as the back edge of the club sole bounces on the sand at contact.

Posture
Stand high, with the knees only very slightly flexed and with your weight centred. Keep the hands in line with the ball, with the club open and, of course, not in contact with the sand.

Aim slightly to the left, as the open club face will cause the ball to curve to the right in the air.

Movement
Make a smooth and controlled backswing followed by an unhurried downswing that allows the club to bounce at impact on the back edge of its sole, as you continue to a full and well-balanced finish.

PLAYING WINNING SHOTS FROM THE SAND

As we said at the beginning of this chapter, courage and confidence are necessary with sand shots, and these will only increase if you practise regularly. You must be able to play bunker shots well enough to avoid losing a stroke, so be sure to spend at least some time every week in the practice bunker.

Wood shots from a fairway bunker
If the ball is lying well in a fairway bunker, the sand is not too soft and there is a low lip between the ball and the target, you may consider using a lofted wood.

1. With the ball in the centre of the stance, hold the club so that the face is open and not in contact with the sand. The right foot is angled strongly so that the inside presses into the sand.

The table opposite sums up the most important points in this chapter. It is a handy guide for quick reference when the ball has landed in normal sand in a greenside bunker and you are considering what to do. The table indicates what swing movement is required when playing from good, half-buried and buried lies.

Remember that you cannot ground your club in a sand bunker without being penalised, and the only way you can feel the texture of the sand is when you walk into the bunker and take your stance.

2. The backswing is slightly shorter and steeper than for a fairway wood shot due to the lack of leg movement (caused by the right ankle position).

3. The arms continue freely into the follow through, the weight being pulled over on to the left leg and the lower body turning towards the target.

Ready-reckoner for bunker play

LIE	STANCE	SWING
Good	Ball in line with left instep, club open, feet, hips and shoulder point to left as much as the club is open to the right. Weight centred.	Free, easy swing with plenty of wrist break. Full follow through. Light grip. 'Slow motion' swing.
Half-buried	Ball well inside the left heel, club and feet square to target. Weight favours left foot.	Free swing with wrists broken earlier than before. Firmer grip.
Buried	Ball back in the stance, club closed, feet, hips and shoulders point to right as much as club is closed to the left.	Firm, resolute grip, wrists break immediately, sharp downswing with right hand pushing into sand. The swing is a strong movement.

CHAPTER NINE
RECOVERY SHOTS FROM THE ROUGH

One of the most disappointing and anxious moments on the golf course is when you have to stand and watch your tee shot move off line and disappear into the rough. By the time you have walked to the ball, your disappointment has turned into anger or despair, and so your chances of playing a good recovery shot are very slim indeed!

The first step in getting out of the rough is to find the ball. Frustration at the result of your shot can lead you to turn away towards your bag without taking a line on the ball by noting a particular mark where it entered the rough. It is vital to keep your eye on the ball until it has gone out of sight, then take a line on that point and make for it as soon as possible.

Once you have found the ball (and checked that it is actually yours – you are in a difficult enough situation without having to incur a penalty stroke for playing the wrong ball), you must decide whether to play the ball as it lies or to declare it unplayable. The lie of the ball and any obstacles between the ball and your target will dictate the choice of club and the swing necessary.

If the grass is thick there is a danger of getting too much of it between the club head and the ball. Another danger is a lack of conservatism – you pick a club with far too little loft and then try to hit the ball too far, usually ending up worse than before.

Be conservative about your choice of club and target, so that even if your strike is less than perfect, the ball will end up back on the fairway, leaving you an easier next shot.

A few examples of typical rough situations will help explain the problems involved and show you how to play the best possible recovery shot.

FROM A GOODISH LIE IN SEMI-ROUGH

Your ball is lying quite well in the semi-rough some 120 yds (110 m) from the green. There is very little rough between your ball and the target. Any loss of length caused by the rough will probably be compensated for by the fact that the ball will fly out with very little back-spin, so that it rolls well after bouncing. Take the same club as you would for this distance if the ball was on the fairway.

Grip
Adopt your normal grip for this situation. Make sure you hold the club lightly but firmly, leaving the mandatory $^1/_2$ in (12 mm) of the shaft above your hands.

Stance
Take the normal width of stance for this length of shot, but the weight should be favouring the left side, while the hands should be slightly more in front of the ball than usual – this is to avoid catching the grass on the backswing. Place the club head very carefully behind the ball, which should be slightly left of centre in the stance.

From a goodish lie in semi-rough

Even when in the rough, your pre-shot routine must always be the same.

1. Having decided on the shot to be played and chosen the club (here a No. 7 iron is best), stand behind the ball and choose the intermediate target.

Posture

Stand with your weight forwards on the balls of the feet and with very little knee flex. The body should be square to the intended flight line.

Swing movement

Swing the club smoothly away from the ball, cocking the wrists early. This helps to create a steeper club-head approach to the ball, ensuring that as little grass as possible is caught between the club head and the ball.

It is essential that the swing remains smooth. Any 'violence' will dig the club head into the ground before the ball is struck. Swing freely with both arms, which will help to ensure that the swing path at impact is pointing at the target and the club face is square to the target line. Continue the swing to a full follow through.

Good timing and balance will prevent you from rushing this shot, so your results from the semi-rough should be no worse than those played from the fairway.

2. Take up the stance with the weight favouring the left side and the hands in front of the ball, which is just left of centre. This is to avoid catching the grass first.

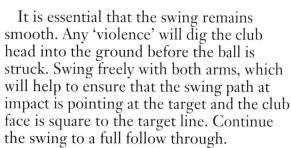

3. A smooth, slow, rather steep backswing with soft hands will enable you to deliver the club head to the ball from a steeper angle than normal with this club.

4. After impact, the left arm continues forwards and to the inside, with the upper body remaining behind the ball's position at address. This creates extension through the ball, preventing the right side from dominating.

5. The swing continues to the follow-through position, bringing the head round by the natural turning of the body so that the eyes are on the ball as it flies to the target.

THICK ROUGH

Play this shot badly and you will probably have to add three or four strokes to your score, you may lose the ball in even deeper rough, and you can certainly end up losing your temper!

When you get to the ball, identify it and examine the lie carefully. Don't anticipate miracles, but pick a highly realistic target for the shot, then choose your club conservatively.

Your first priority when considering how to play a shot like this is to get the ball back on to the fairway, where your next shot will be much more straightforward. Under no circumstances should your next shot have to be played from the rough too, so you have to decide if you want to go for the green or if a simple shot that gets you sensibly back on the fairway is the better choice. My advice is that if you have any doubt whatsoever about your chances of reaching the green, let discretion be the better part of valour and play the ball safely back on to the fairway.

Your shot must make the ball rise sharply to prevent the long grass from impeding its flight too much. Therefore, choose a lofted club, either the No. 9 iron, the pitching wedge or the sand iron. The heavily-flanged sand iron is often best.

Grip
Place the hands further down the shaft than usual and with the right hand placed more to the left on top of the left thumb. This prevents the club face from closing too early, leaving too little loft on the club. Hold the club firmly with both hands.

Stance
With the ball well back in the stance, the feet should be wider apart than when playing the lofted club from a normal lie. Your weight should be well on the left foot and the hands in front of the ball.

Posture
Lean forwards, weight on the balls of the feet. The left foot should be withdrawn from the target line so that the stance is open. The lower body should be open also (pointing to the left of the target line).

From thick rough back to the fairway

1. A ball has been found – but is it the right ball? First identify, then get down to work. What can be done here?

2. There is no question about it, the sensible thing to do is to play the ball back on to the fairway so that the next shot will be easier.

3. The sand iron is the best club for this job. Hold the club with the face square but with the right hand turned slightly to the left on the shaft to prevent the club face from closing too soon.

Swing movement

The address position for this shot is similar to that for the normal sand shot, except for the position of the right hand on the club and the strength of grip. However, for this shot from the thick rough, the club is swung steeply with a strong arm movement up to a three-quarter backswing, then down to the ball with the weight on the left foot all the time. Make a great effort to ensure that the club keeps moving after impact.

Although this is a strong swing movement, keep in mind that precision and a correct strike are vital in order to fly the ball the required distance out of the rough. However strongly you swing the club, the swing must be smooth and rhythmical, otherwise too much power will be lost before the club head strikes the ball.

Take care that you don't hit the ball so hard that it flies out of the rough, over the fairway, and into the rough on the other side.

It is not often that you see players practising shots out of the rough. They should!

4. After a couple of practice swings, address the ball carefully so as not to disturb the position of the ball. Even here, you must have a target and an intermediate target. You don't want this shot to end in worse rough or in the water! (*Left*)

5. A steep backswing with plenty of early hand movement helps to create a descending blow on the downswing. (*Right*)

6. Both arms swing *through* the ball and not at it, and the left arm continues the movement all the way. (*Left*)

7. The follow through is completed and in the finish position the ball can be watched all the time until it comes to rest. (*Right*)

FROM THE ROUGH OVER OR BETWEEN TREES

There will undoubtedly be occasions when the ball not only lands in inhospitable rough but you find that there are high bushes or even trees between you and the fairway. Check the lie carefully. Can you play a safe shot back the way the ball came in to the rough, so that you are at least safely on the fairway? If not, then you have to play between or over those trees.

If you go for a between-the-trees shot, there must be plenty of room between them to provide a margin of error. A shot that hits a tree is not only dangerous but can also leave the ball further back in the rough, and you will be worse off than before. Make full use of your intermediate

Between the trees from the rough

When you choose to play the ball low between the trees, pick the club out first and then concentrate on the all-important aim. A club that is too lofted can send the ball into the tree-tops.

1. Examine the situation very carefully: the lie of the ball, the space between the trees, and then choose the shot – a punch shot (*see* pp. 90 – 1) with a half swing.

2. Take practice swings to give the right feel for the shot, holding the club firmly with both hands well down the shaft, with the weight mainly on the left foot. Imagine the successful flight of the ball.

3. Place the club very carefully behind the ball, checking on the intermediate target and seeing the desired flight. The hands are well in front of the ball, which is back in the stance.

4. The arms have swung down through the ball, the left arm leading, with little wrist action. The arms will now rotate to prevent the ball lifting too much.

target to ensure that your aim is correct.

Playing over the trees is very difficult if the ball is lying badly, so think carefully before deciding what to do. (You can always declare the ball unplayable, with one penalty stroke added to your score.) Should you decide to play over the trees, you must bring your imagination into play.

During your practice swings (don't take them too near the ball or you may cause it to move), imagine the flight of the ball, seeing in your mind's eye how you successfully lift it the required height.

A full follow through to a balanced finish is important when playing this high shot.

Over the trees from the rough

1. Stand behind the ball and consider the options. Is it best to play it back out on to the fairway, between the trees or over them? If the choice is over, then the most lofted club, the sand iron, is the one to use.

2. Having picked out the intermediate target, take a practice swing, visualising the flight of the ball over the trees to a successful conclusion.

3. Using the intermediate target to align the club head, place it very carefully behind the ball. Take the stance and once again visualise the ball flight over the trees.

4. Make a half backswing, cocking the wrists early to make the club rise steeply to avoid getting too much grass between the club head and the ball. (*Left*)

5. Swing the club down at the back of the ball with the left arm leading to ensure the continued swing and good balance. Watch the ball very carefully on the follow through as it is easy to misjudge distance when you are concentrating on creating maximum height. (*Right*)

THE LONG SHOT FROM THE SEMI-ROUGH

When the ball is in semi-rough, the lofted wood (a No. 5 or No. 6 wood) is often a good choice, especially if it has a ribbed sole that helps it glide along the grass without losing any of its speed. (The lofted wood is sometimes the better club to use even in the thick rough, if the ball is lying reasonably, because it will glide through the grass, whereas an iron often gets grass wrapped around its hosel before impact.)

The grip, stance and posture are the same as for the normal fairway wood shot, except that you play the ball a little further back in the stance and the grip is shortened. These two changes result in a more downward blow, ensuring that the ball is struck first and the ground afterwards.

The swing movement is also exactly the same as that for the normal wood shot from the fairway – smooth and unhurried, with a full follow through leading to a perfectly balanced finish position.

Should the ball be sitting up on top of the rough grass, you can play the shot as a tee shot (*see* Chapter Seven); that is, with a less-lofted wood, the ball further forwards in the stance, and with more weight on the right foot at address.

Remember when playing this shot that you should not ground the club behind the ball, as this may make the ball move, inflicting a penalty stroke. Hold the club off the grass when assuming the address position.

When playing shots from the rough, precision is more important than power, so swing smoothly through the ball to a full finish with the hands high and the whole body in balance. This will enhance contact between ball and club head; as we know, the better the strike, the better the result. Look at the ball and swing the club freely, with the arms and hands, allowing the body to react to the swinging of the club. It's not always tough in the rough!

From the semi-rough with a lofted wood _____

1. When there is a considerable distance left to the target from the semi-rough, play the more lofted wood. Here, the No. 5 wood is played with a shortened grip and the ball centred in the stance.

2. Swing the club smoothly away from the ball into the backswing.

3. The ball is on its way and the arms continue freely, with the upper body behind the ball's position at address.

4. The arms have pulled the upper body round to the correct finish position, with the left side well through, and a perfect balance.

AFTERWORD

If you have read through this book and followed the exercises and advice in it, your golf will have improved step by step. If you have played as often as you can and practised regularly, you are certainly more at home with your game than you were when you started. But no matter how well you are doing, it is all too easy to stray from the straight and narrow path of good golf and get lost in the wilderness of hooks and slices!

In order to maintain any standard of proficiency at any level of excellence, you must practise regularly. Also, good practice helps to get rid of bad golfing habits and increases confidence in your ability – in itself a huge asset when endeavouring to play better golf.

Practice versus playing

There is an immense difference between practising and playing golf. When you practise you want to maintain or improve some specific part of your game; for instance you want to 're-program' your golfing mind to the amount of backswing necessary to play a simple pitch from 30 yds/m on to the green, or you want to improve your long-putting ability, so that your long putt leaves you with a simple putt to hole out. When you play, however, you have a different aim – you want to move the ball from tee to hole with the lowest number of strokes. So let's start with practising first!

How and when to practise

Always decide beforehand what element of your game you want to practise. Preferably, choose one element per session, and concentrate on the change that you are trying to make, not on the immediate result of the attempt.

If possible, find a spot with good turf where you will be on your own, so that you can concentrate completely on the task in hand and you won't feel embarrassed if your first attempts are not successful. Go

Write down the results of each practice session in a notebook. This will help you chart your improvement, which will be of great assistance should your swing changes need reinforcement in the future.

through your warming-up exercises and then hit two or three balls with a short iron to get the right feel, with good timing and a clean strike. Even here, do not neglect your pre-swing routine. Place a ball a couple of club lengths in the direction of the target; this is your intermediate target.

Now, say you are trying to improve your three-quarter swing from a good lie. Make sure that all your swings from now on are three-quarter swings. This goes too for the practice swings that you take as part of your pre-swing routine. Every swing you make must conform with that which you are trying to improve. You often see people practising with the whole range of clubs in the bag. That is bad practice. Furthermore, your pre-swing routine should also include, time and again, the same elements: seeing the successful flight of the ball during the practice swings, grip, stance, posture, waggles and forward press. In other words, the same routine as always: you practise as you play, and you play as you practise.

It is essential that you have a clear picture in your mind of what you want to achieve with each practice session. While practising this particular part of your game, you must be prepared for the fact that your striking ability is going to deteriorate. Don't get upset at this – it is quite natural because you are concentrating on just one of the elements of your swing, not on the whole swing. When you practise you think of the swing from the ball and then back to the ball; when you play, you think from the ball to the target.

Move away every time you play a shot, consider the result and then start again, going through a constant routine. Make your practice session a series of, say, ten balls each time, with a short break in between, while you write down the results in your notebook, bearing in mind the nine ball-flight alternatives we have already discussed in the cause-and-effect table in Chapter One. We give here the same table, but we leave out the cause and add a remedy instead.

EFFECT OF YOUR SWING	REMEDY
1 The ball flies in a straight line towards the target.	Well done! Keep on doing what you're doing. If we could all do that all the time, we professional golf instructors would go out of business.
2 It flies in a straight line to the left of the target.	Move the ball further back in the stance. Make sure to swing down on the inside of the target line.
3 It flies in a straight line to the right of the target.	Move the ball further forwards in the stance. Make sure to clear the left hip at impact.
4 It starts off straight to the target and then curves to the left.	Move the hands to the left on the shaft and/or increase the pressure exerted by the right hand.
5 It starts off straight to the target and then curves to the right.	Move the hands to the right on the shaft and/or reduce the pressure exerted by the right hand.
6 It starts off to the left of the target line and then curves back to the right.	Two things to correct! Move the hands to the right of the shaft. Then place the ball further back in the stance and swing the club down on the inside to along the target line at impact and then back to the inside.
7 It starts off to the left of the target line and then curves more to the left.	Again, two things to correct. Move the hands to the left on the shaft. Then move the ball further back in the stance and make sure to swing down on the inside path.
8 It starts off to the right of the target line and then curves back to the left.	Two things to correct. Move the hands to the left on the shaft. Then place the ball further forwards in the stance. Clear the left hip early on the downswing.
9 It starts off to the right of the target line and then curves to the right.	Two things to correct. Move the hands to the right on the shaft. Then move the ball further forwards in the stance. Clear the left hip at impact.

How much further forwards or back in the stance you should move the ball is something that you have to work out for yourself by trial and error.

Start again and play another series of ten balls, making any adjustments that you consider necessary, before taking another pause and noting any changes in the result.

Nothing is so tiring as concentrated practice, especially if it doesn't result in immediate improvement, so don't practise for too long in the beginning. Otherwise, tiredness and lack of concentration in the latter part of your session may ruin the good work you have done in the early part.

It is better to practise three or four times a week for a short while than to practise for two hours once a week .

Don't make things too difficult for yourself – if for instance you are practising full swings with your No. 4 iron and it is simply not working, then hit some successful shots with your No. 5 iron or even your No. 6 iron, to build up your confidence. Then play a few shots with the No. 4 again, go back to the No. 5 for another couple of confidence stiffeners, and so on until you are again playing that stroke confidently with your No. 4 iron.

When you have completed practising the relevant element in your game and have noted any changes that have occurred in ball-flight behaviour, finish off with about ten minutes doing something that you know you enjoy doing and know that you do well – chipping, putting or whatever – anything that will make you leave the practice area with a feeling of satisfaction and achievement.

What to practise
Golf knowledge and understanding come only with time and experience. Reading books or watching an instructional video or a televised tournament will surely help a great deal, but at best they only complement good personal instruction from your golf pro. In legal circles, there is an axiom that says, 'He who acts as his own lawyer has a fool for a client'. So it is with golf. We all need help some time or other – even the tournament players – and no one is better equipped to help you than your club professional. After all, that is his job, but he does need your assistance. Don't just ask for one lesson – it is usually necessary for two or three before you rid yourself of a fault or create a solid improvement. Everyone can see that you are doing *something* wrong, many can see *what* you are doing wrong, but only your pro knows *why*!

Don't try to impress the pro; he has seen far too many swings to be impressed. For the same reason, never be embarrassed by indifferent performance. Changes to your swing are often uncomfortable and take time, so let your pro decide the pace, duration and spacing of the lessons.

Bad practice is something that we see far too often, with many people using a tremendous number of golf balls and playing them badly with all the different clubs. These people do not improve their golf, they simply ingrain their mistakes, which then will be much more difficult to get rid of.

Practise the shorter and easier swing movements first, but make sure that your swing tempo during practice is the same as that used when you are out on the course. If it is different, the good swing movement will not be encouraged. Neither should you be stopping during the swing to check the position of the club head, as this will make your swing become very position-oriented.

So practise one thing at a time, taking the simpler movements first, noting your changes and improvements as you go along in order to be able to refer to these notes if you need to reinforce these changes at a later date.

Practice sessions should take place when you are at your leisure. If you have a guilty feeling that you should be somewhere else, your practice is not going to be effective. (The same thing can be said about actually playing – always plan your golf round when you have enough free time to be able to enjoy yourself in a properly relaxed way.)

Practice seems to do most good when you are not planning to go out and play a round afterwards. In other words, your best practice takes place when you come to the club just to practise and when you have taken a lesson the day before.

Many of us just don't have the time to get out to the club too often and so have to practise before we go out on a round. When practising just before playing, you must concentrate on a basic element of your game: for instance, swing tempo, balance, arm freedom or pre-swing routine, not on any specific problems that you have at the time. You won't be able to correct a specific problem in the thirty minutes before you tee off. If you notice that your swing is producing a fade, don't try to change it, but accept that that is the shot that you will be playing for the day, and plan for it by adjusting swing path and club-face position prior to playing. Last-minute changes to your established swing should never be made out on the course.

The better player you are, the more likely you are to practise after playing to repair any faults that have become apparent during the round, while they are fresh in your mind. But even then, have only one particular element of your game in mind, give every shot full concentration, play only a few balls in each series, and rest and think in between.

Playing versus practising

The following are some of the main differences between playing and practising. You only get one chance for every shot out on the course and the result of that shot affects how you must play the next. At the end of the day, you have every stroke – good, bad and indifferent – in black and white on your scorecard. Add to this any nervousness you might feel, who your playing partners are, what the weather is like, and if you are comfortable with the particular course being played. Many problems, if you let yourself think in those terms, but successful players at all levels find them a very enjoyable challenge.

So look forward to meeting your playing partners, determine to do only what you feel you are capable of doing and come well prepared, having checked the night before that you have everything you need: glove, umbrella, balls, tees, green repairer, pencil, etc.

After warming and loosening up (*see* pp. 56–7), play a few practice three-quarter shots with the No. 8 or No. 9 iron to instil confidence and to encourage correct striking from the beginning. Then play a few three-quarter swings with the medium irons, and finally about half a dozen full swings with a wood. Note the ball trajectory and the shape of the ball flight. Don't try to change anything, because this is going to be your shot all day and you must plan each stroke on the course accordingly. Finish off this little pre-game session with a few pitches and a few chips, before really quietening down with some medium-long putts. N.B. Don't attempt any

When choosing a spot to tee up the ball, look for a flat piece of ground for both the ball and your feet. Remember that it is not necessary to tee up right at the front of the tee; you will probably find the ground in much better condition two club lengths back.

short putts before playing – if you miss a few it won't do your confidence any good at all.

Then off you go to the first tee to get off to a successful start. Pick out the target area before placing the ball on the tee. Make a few loosening-up movements with the club (not full swings) to work up a feeling for the smoothness and rhythm that your shot requires, seeing all the while a successful result. Go through your pre-swing routine and play the shot exactly as you have visualised it, straight over the intermediate target on the correct trajectory, landing and bouncing to a stop where you planned, leaving you with an easy second shot. Excellent! We're going to have fun today!

During practice, you think of segments of your swing. Out on the course, you feel the wholeness of the swing, its rhythm and balance, and its fine finish position. When you practise you think, and when you play you feel.